Thinking, Learning & Succeeding in the Community College

Christopher L. Rand
Lynn J. Lessie

THOMSON

Australia · Canada · Mexico · Singapore · Spain · United Kingdom · United States

Thinking, Learning & Succeeding in the Community College
Christopher L. Rand/ Lynn J. Lessie

Executive Editors:
Michele Baird, Maureen Staudt &
Michael Stranz

Project Development Manager:
Linda de Stefano

Marketing Coordinators:
Lindsay Annett and Sara Mercurio

Production/Manufacturing Supervisor:
Donna M. Brown

Pre-Media Services Supervisor:
Dan Plofchan

Rights and Permissions Specialists:
Kalina Hintz and Bahman Naraghi

Cover Image
Getty Images*

The Adaptable Courseware Program
consists of products and additions to
existing Thomson products that are
produced from camera-ready copy.
Peer review, class testing, and
accuracy are primarily the responsibility
of the author(s).

Library of Congress Control Number:
2006905457

Thinking, Learning & Succeeding in the
Community College / Christopher L.
Rand/ & Lynn J. Lessie – First Edition
p. 220
ISBN 0-759-39127-0

International Divisions List

Asia (Including India):
Thomson Learning
(a division of Thomson Asia Pte Ltd)
5 Shenton Way #01-01
UIC Building
Singapore 068808
Tel: (65) 6410-1200
Fax: (65) 6410-1208

Australia/New Zealand:
Thomson Learning Australia
102 Dodds Street
Southbank, Victoria 3006
Australia

Latin America:
Thomson Learning
Seneca 53
Colonia Polano
11560 Mexico, D.F., Mexico
Tel (525) 281-2906
Fax (525) 281-2656

Canada:
Thomson Nelson
1120 Birchmount Road
Toronto, Ontario
Canada M1K 5G4
Tel (416) 752-9100
Fax (416) 752-8102

UK/Europe/Middle East/Africa:
Thomson Learning
High Holborn House
50-51 Bedford Row
London, WC1R 4L$
United Kingdom
Tel 44 (020) 7067-2500
Fax 44 (020) 7067-2600

Spain (Includes Portugal):
Thomson Paraninfo
Calle Magallanes 25
28015 Madrid
España
Tel 34 (0)91 446-3350
Fax 34 (0)91 445-6218

CREDITS

This page constitutes an extension of the copyright page. We have made every effort to trace the ownership of all copyrighted material and to secure permission from copyright holders. In the event of any question arising as to the use of any material, we will be pleased to make the necessary corrections in future printings. Thanks are due to the following authors, publishers, and agents for permission to use the material indicated.

TABLE OF CONTENTS

A MESSAGE FROM THE AUTHORS

This book was designed for your use in Atlantic Cape Community College's course, DEVS 111, College Skills. The goals of this course are:

- To develop skills and learning strategies that will lead to academic success in college courses.
- To support the learning of your linked psychology or sociology course with analysis and review of the text and lecture material, the use of study groups, and the application of the study skills and learning strategies.
- To increase critical thinking skills through a series of thinking and writing activities.

The book is divided into two parts. In Part I, specific study skills that are crucial for success in college are presented. You may know some of these already but college-level work requires careful and consistent use of these skills. And there are many that you probably have not tried before. You will complete a variety of exercises that will build some of these essential skills. Your performance in this and all your courses will improve.

Part II is devoted to the development of critical thinking skills. Each assignment in this section includes exercises that are completed weekly. The activities will guide you through a series of increasingly more difficult reading, analysis and writing assignments that will increase your critical thinking skills. As you complete these assignments, you will be working on progressively higher levels of intellectual and academic activities. The critical thinking skills of interpretation, analysis, evaluation and application of knowledge to new situations are essential for success in college courses.

We could not put the most important things in this book: your motivation and determination. If you contribute those, the hints and exercises found in this book will assure you a productive and fulfilling academic career. We wish you success in this and all your college courses.

Prof. Christopher Rand   Prof. Lynn Lessie

Getting Started

Introduction

In this chapter, you will get to know your college and some of the basic expectations of the college. You will find out what kinds of degrees are offered, what the general and specific requirements are for your major, what learning resources are available. You will begin to organize your time so you can accomplish the work of the semester. You will calculate a GPA. Finally, you will begin the process of critical thinking.

Goals

After you have completed the work in this chapter, you will
- Enjoy a level of familiarity with the college
- Know who and what resources can help remove obstacles
- Begin a process to organize your time and reduce stress
- Become aware of incomplete and biased information that interferes with thinking

Activities/Tasks

These are the steps you need to take in order to complete the activities in the chapter. You should check off as you complete each activity or task.

1. Study the catalog and course listings for general education_____
2. Review the requirements for your major_____
3. Visit at least three resources on campus (ACTION)_____
4. Calculate a GPA_____
5. Develop a time management plan/stress reduction plan_____
6. Implement a stress reduction activity_____
7. Read, think about, and respond to the critical thinking exercise._____
8. Answer or add at least one general knowledge question_____

Learning Objectives

These are the assignments you need to complete and show or hand in to your instructor. You will:

1. Use the college catalog and participate in a discussion about the requirements for each type of degree and the requirements for a major (or majors you are interested in.
2. Share and submit a statement about three resources on campus, describing the function of each.
3. Calculate, and submit, a GPA and realize the importance of maintaining an adequate GPA.
4. Submit an analysis of your time management journal, following the directions of the instructor.
5. Begin critical thinking by assessing statements for objectivity, bias, and completeness.
6. Contribute to the general knowledge fund.

Chapter 1: An Introduction to College

WHAT TO EXPECT AS YOU START COLLEGE

Going to college is a major step in your life. Whatever your reasons, you've made a choice to sacrifice your time and energy to get a higher education. Not only have you chosen to make your life more complicated, in most cases you'll also be paying for it with your time and probably with your money, regardless of financial aid. So, why put yourself through such an ordeal? The answer may be as simple as the fact that getting a college education leads to a better and higher paying job, which is true. It could be that others in your family have told you that going to college is the best thing for you if you want to "make something of yourself." Whether it is money or just something others tell you is necessary, the most important aspect of going and adjusting to college is that you take full responsibility for your education. Make sure you want it for yourself. You will be the one who makes decisions about studying and learning. You will be the one who has to put the energy and concentration into the work. You're the one who will face the stress and anxiety of tests and papers. You must be prepared to make a major commitment.

A POSITIVE ATTITUDE

Like any other endeavor you will face in life, it will be necessary for you to work and have a positive attitude to do well. You need to build your confidence in your academic skills and learn how to become an active learner. Unlike high school, you will have to provide the motivation for your learning. There will be nobody at college who will force you to go to class or to complete your assignments. In some classes, attendance may not be mandatory (although all professors prefer that students attend), so it will be up to you to get out of bed or to turn off the TV and get to class.

Not only will you have to attend classes physically, but you must be prepared to come to class ready to learn. If you are going to your classes and you are sleeping through them or day-dreaming, you might as well stay home and sleep where it's more comfortable. Sleeping through class is not the way to get the professor on your

side. Even if they don't say anything to you, they know when you are paying attention. Be prepared to go to school and be alert.

THE TRAPS OF TIME:

Trap #1: PROCRASTINATION

It is very easy to put off studying or doing assignments, particularly when you are anxious about them in the first place. However, one of the biggest reasons that students do poorly in school is because they don't study until the last second. Everything is in the future. Putting it off does alleviate the fear for the moment, but it catches up to you. When you don't give yourself enough time to do your best work, you usually end up with a second rate product. Help yourself. Go over each class's syllabus thoroughly. Find out when exams or projects are due and get a jump on them.

Trap #2: TOO MUCH TIME

One disturbing thing about going to college is that it will force you to rearrange your time schedule. It is a little different than what you remember from your high school days. You attended classes at your high school for about six hours a day, five days a week, at the very least. In college, you're probably going to class three or four days a week for a total of between 12 – 16 hours per week. This does not seem like much time. You may or may not have had to put a lot of time or effort in the books while you were in high school, but in college you are expected to do the bulk of your academic work outside the classroom. It may seem as though you have time to get your projects done or to begin studying for that first exam if they are weeks away, yet most students find that if they were not working from day one of the class they should have been. Don't let time get away from you. Use every available hour to get your education on track.

Trap #3: TOO LITTLE TIME

On the other hand, some students come to college, especially community college, and they think they have no time for school. The natural question that comes to them is, "Why am I here?" They know they need a college education to get ahead, but they don't know how they are going to fit it into their schedule. So, they fit in the time it takes to go to classes, but not the time to study and do their best work. For many of these students, college becomes a frustrating and unachievable goal. When it comes to time, you need to be realistic. You should ask yourself these questions: Can I do a good job at work and still be a full-time student? Will the job allow me to have a flexible schedule when exams are coming? Will I have enough time for my family and friends? If the answer to any of these questions is no, your best bet is to start slowly. You should begin your college education by taking just one class to see what it takes to succeed. You will then be able to make judgments about the amount of time you can devote to taking classes.

KNOW YOUR COLLEGE

Perhaps the biggest barrier to achieving success in college is not in understanding how it works. Even a small community college has its own bureaucracy, which makes rules and regulations that can affect your college career. The following are ways of getting information about your school and how it works, from choosing your professors and classes to finding help when you need it.

The Catalogue

Most college catalogues, which are usually printed each year, contain much of the general information you will need to know about your institution. The catalog will give a description of the departments and the services that are available to students. They will contain information about the types of degrees and give descriptions of courses you will need to take to complete a particular degree. It is important to note that the catalogue will also tell you how many credits are needed to complete a particular degree. Most community colleges require between 62 and 66 credits to graduate. Therefore, if you are taking 12 credits a semester (which is the least you can take and still be full time for financial aide purposes) then it will take you more than two years to graduate, unless you attend summer sessions or increase the number of credits you take in later semesters. In Figure 1-1, you can see a comparison between two full-time schedules. Each schedule is appropriate. The two year model demands much more time from you than the 12 credit model. You will probably be taking more courses each semester in the two year model which makes it more difficult for most students. There are other variations or models you can use, but you need to make decisions about how much time you want to spend before graduating.

FIGURE 1-1

An Associate's degree from most community colleges requires approximately 64 credits to graduate. The chart below shows a comparison between a student taking a full time schedule at 12 credits per semester and a student taking enough credits during the year to graduate in two years.

12 CREDIT MODEL

Freshman year
semester one	12 credits
semester two	12 credits
	24 credits

Sophomore year
semester three	12 credits
semester four	12 credits
	24 credits

Total credits needed to graduate	64
Total credits earned	48
additional credits needed	16

2 YEAR GRADUATION MODEL

Freshman year
semester one	12 credits
semester two	16 credits
summer session	4 credits
	32 credits

Sophomore year
semester three	16 credits
semester four	16 credits
	32 credits

Credits needed to graduate	64
Credits earned	64
Additional credits needed	0

The college catalog will also give you course descriptions telling you generally what will be covered in specific classes. It may also have a listing of the full-time professors and their academic credentials. This is important to know.

Many community colleges have a large portion of their classes taught by adjunct instructors. Because many of them teach for only a few semesters, it is very difficult for colleges to provide students with each adjunct's education and experience. Knowing the backgrounds of the professors will allow you to make decisions concerning what sections you will register for in a particular class. Most catalogs also have a calendar, which gives important dates throughout the school year, such as the beginning and end of the semester or the dates when final exams are given.

Student Calendar and Handbook

The student handbook or calendar contains material similar to the catalogue but might contain other information which is also important. Many student handbooks give the names, titles and photos of faculty and staff on campus, particularly the people in the Student Services Department. The Student Service area is usually composed of people who directly work with students and student problems, such as counselors or financial aid personnel. The Student Handbook will also discuss the fundamental rules and regulations of the college. For example, it might describe the policy for drinking alcoholic beverages on campus or explain how to obtain a parking sticker for on-campus parking. The Student Handbook will also highlight important dates on the school calendar like the final day to withdraw and not receive an F or the day an incomplete grade from the past semester turns into an F.

HOW TO CALCULATE A GRADE POINT AVERAGE

You can't play the game if you don't know how to keep score. Knowing your Grade Point Average (GPA), will help you to make decisions about how well you are doing in school. Most community colleges expect students to maintain a minimum GPA of 2.0, which at most institutions is a C average. There may be some leniency in the Freshman-year, but in most cases if a student is unable to achieve a 2.0 after a year (2 semesters), he or she will be put on some type of academic probation. If the student does not improve his or her GPA in the following semesters, this may lead to dismissal from the college. Some community colleges will allow the student to continue on a part- time basis (fewer than 12 credits), or will let them try again after a prescribed period of time.

The GPA also plays a major role when trying to transfer to a senior institution. Most four year colleges want students to graduate from a community college with a 3.0 GPA or B average. Many senior institutions will waive the need for an SAT (Scholastic Aptitude Test) score or other type of predictive test if they see that a student has demonstrated appropriate academic achievement at a community college.

It makes sense to know how to calculate your GPA. Most two year institutions use a quality point system based around the A, B, C, D, F grading system. Using this system, an instructor will give a grade of A, B, C, D, or F at the end of each semester. There are other grade possibilities which we will discuss later in the chapter, but A, B, C, D and F are the basic grades. Each of these grades is then assigned a numerical value. For example A = 4, B = 3, C = 2, D = 1, F = 0. The numerical equivalent of the grade is then multiplied by the number of credits that are assigned to a particular course. Credits are the value of the course which measures progress toward graduation. Credits are usually based on the number of hours that the class meets per week. After the credits are multiplied each of the totals from all classes taken that semester are added up. The total of this sum is then divided by the total number of credits taken that semester. The following is a sample of how to calculate your grade point average.

FIGURE 1-2

Course	Cred/Course	Grade #		equivalent		total
ENGLISH	3	A	x	4	=	12
MATH	3	B	x	3	=	9
HISTORY	3	C	x	2	=	6
BIOLOGY	+ 4	C	x	2	=	+ 8
Sums	13					35

Divide the sum of the credits I course into the sum of the total column.

$$
\begin{array}{r}
2.69 = \text{GPA} \\
13\overline{)35.00} \\
\underline{26} \\
90 \\
\underline{78} \\
1\,20 \\
\underline{1\,17} \\
3
\end{array}
$$

13

RESOURCES ON CAMPUS

Most community colleges have many departments that are designed specifically to help the student succeed. The types of services available range from helping the student with academic problems to services that provide personal support for the student. Many of these services can be found by contacting the Dean of Students' office or by checking with a college counselor. The most common services and their uses are as follows:

The Library

The library is where the majority of the college's books and periodicals are housed. The collection of books probably contains fiction and nonfiction, textbooks, and reference books. The periodicals may range from a number of daily newspapers to monthly journals that deal with specific disciplines or areas of academic study. The key to finding books or other material in the library is to understand the catalog system used by the college. Most colleges use the Library of Congress catalog system which may be different than the one you used in high school. To learn how to use this catalog system, ask the librarian. They usually have a tour or provide a specific training tool to help new students. The library may also employ electronic reference material such as CD ROM referencing services. This again may be different from what you have experienced in the past; if you're not familiar with the technology, ask the librarian for assistance.

Computer Labs

Most community colleges now have several computer labs that are designated for student use. The word processing component of the computer is the most commonly used function but there are several other features that may be helpful including a database or spread sheet programs.

Computer competency is a must for today's student. It simplifies the writing process greatly. Computer labs provide computers that have additional features such as spell and grammar checking devices. These features take a great deal of the pressure off the writer. Make sure that you familiarize yourself with the computer and the labs as early in the semester as possible.

Writing and Math Labs

Community colleges usually have specialized labs that are open to students who need help in math or writing. These labs are designed so students can walk in and get help on specific assignments or with problems they are having in a particular area. These labs are generally staffed by paraprofessionals or student tutor. Most labs are cost free and can be of great value if you are having a problem in math or with writing assignments. The trick with using labs effectively is getting to them before a problem becomes too overwhelming. Too many times students know that they are in trouble in a class but are reluctant to get help. Using the college's resources is the sign of a smart student. If you think you are in trouble, you probably are. Get help!

Learning Disability Service

If you have been diagnosed as learning disabled or are willing to be tested for a learning disability most colleges will provide you with special services that can help in your education. Some schools provide note takers or people who will assist with lectures. Other times, student service personnel will communicate with your professors and let them know what kinds of things they can do to allow you to succeed, such as giving longer periods of time for test-taking or allowing you to tape record lectures. Even if you haven't been formally diagnosed as learning disabled, but have had problems in the past with certain types of assignments or tests, it is probably in your best interest to discuss this with your professor. They may have alternative methods of evaluating your work.

T.V. Courses and Distance Learning

The age of new technology allows many college courses to be offered away from the campus. This form of gaining credit is for the student who has a very demanding schedule and is unable to take all their courses on campus. In a distance education course, the class usually meets on campus only a few times per semester or not at all. Lectures are generally based around a textbook that is published with an accompanying video tape program or is associated with a public television series that is kept on video. Distance education courses use a course software package. (See Chapter Six) These videos are usually housed in the media department of the college or in the library where students can borrow these tapes for a limited amount of time. In most cases the student only comes on campus for an orientation and to take exams or to turn in assignments. Distance education courses can be a good time saver, but they do present some other problems. The student is left to learn the material alone without the assistance of the professor or other students. For some, this diminishes the worth of the classes. It would be smart not to try one of these courses until you have become comfortable as a student.

A second type of off-campus instruction is called distance learning. This is the wave of the future, where small groups of students take college courses in their homes or in places convenient to where they live. Television hook-ups are placed at these sites and specific classes are presented to small groups across the broadcasting area. Instructors can provide interactive lectures with their students through the use of television. This allows the student and the instructor to see and hear each other from their respective places. The instructor is usually on campus where a broadcast studio is set up.

Tutoring

A tutoring system is in place at most community colleges. This service is usually free and is staffed by paraprofessional teachers or student tutors. The aim of a tutoring service is to give a student who is having a problem with a specific course, some 'one on one' help. You can most likely find a tutor to provide help in any class, from biology to child psychology. Like the writing and math labs, the student must recognize early on in the class that they are in trouble so they can get a tutor before it is too late.

Branch Campuses

Branch campuses are places where a college provides service to their students away from the main campus. The idea behind the branch campus is to be able to give students college services close to their homes. Therefore, many branch campuses are located in areas where there is a high density of students. Sometimes, a branch campus cannot provide all the services of the main campus. Perhaps not all the courses for a particular degree are offered at the branch campus or not all programs are offered at that campus, especially programs that use a lot of technology or need a lot of laboratory time. However, these campuses can usually provide the basic courses needed for most degrees. Using a branch campus can save time and transportation costs. Check to see if there is campus close to you. It might be of some help as you go through school.

STRESS AND HOW TO HANDLE IT

The Signs of Stress

Any time you begin a new task, especially one that you know has some difficulties involved, you will feel a certain amount of stress. Beginning college certainly falls into one of those stress-inducing tasks. There is no way to entirely get rid of this feeling. What you don't want to do is let the stress hurt you physically or emotionally or interfere with achieving your goals. One of the first things you can do to begin handling stress is to recognize when it is affecting you. When you are under stress, you may have feelings of always being rushed or never having enough time. You may become unusually irritable or argue more than normal. Sometimes people under too much stress begin to worry and lose sleep or they become continually tired or listless. Other people feel it physically by having abnormal headaches or indigestion. If any or several of these signs persist over a long time it could be that you are suffering from too much stress.

What Can You Do to Handle Stress

If you have been suffering from some of these symptoms for a long time you may want to consult a physician. But the best way to handle stress is to not let it get out of hand in the first place. The following is a list of techniques that can help you keep stress under control.

- <u>Make sure you budget time for physical activity</u> during your weekly schedule. The exercise will help you to reduce stress. The activity should be something you enjoy.
- <u>Talk about things you're worried about</u>. The ventilation of concerns and feelings will help to reduce stress. Sometimes when you verbalize things that are bothering you, you get a more realistic perspective on them.
- <u>Get rid of things that can cause stress</u>. Put off things that can cause you stress during your school year. Get rid of them. Prioritized your time. This may not be the right time to become president of a club, start a new home project or take on new responsibilities
- <u>Prepare and organize your life</u> as much as possible. Set up routines, make schedules that are achievable and that include time for fun and relaxation.
- <u>Get enough sleep</u>. Understand that when you're tired, you are less effective which is a cause of stress. Most people need between six to eight hours of sleep per night to stay healthy and clearheaded.

- Give yourself a break. Don't be overly critical if everything doesn't go exactly as planned. Know that there are barriers and blockades that will be in your way sometimes. Don't let them get the best of you.
- Try to be happy. You have chosen a path that will ultimately help you. Be proud of yourself. Give yourself a pat on the back. If you can stay happy at least 51% of the time, you are doing well.

TIME MANAGEMENT

One of the most difficult things you will have to do when adjusting to college is to get control of how you use your time. As you will soon realize, your college classes and studying will demand a large portion of your week. As a general rule of thumb, you should spend two hours studying for every hour spent in class. Therefore, if you are taking 12 hours of classes (4 classes that meets 3 hours per week) you should be studying 24 hours per week. Remember, taking 12 credit hours each semester is the minimum amount of credits you can take and still be a full-time student. You will also spend time getting ready to go to your classes and traveling to the campus. All in all, you will probably be using over 40 hours per week or the equivalent of a full-time job in your quest for an education. This makes working full-time and being a full-time student an extremely difficult task. There are only 168 hours in a week and a commitment of at least 80 hours to work and go to school does not leave a lot of time for many other things. Some students can do it, most can not, without letting either their work or their studies suffer.

You will also find that the amount of time you need may vary during the semester. There will be times, when exams or written assignments are due, that you will have to spend even more time on your studies than usual. On many occasions you will find that your professors schedule exams during the same week, usually around the fourth week, the eighth week (midterm exams), the twelfth week and the sixteenth week (final exams). So be sure to check each class's syllabus and see if there will be weeks when exams or papers are due in more than one class. This will allow you to prepare appropriately.

Once you have determined how much time you will need to study and what weeks will be the most time intensive, you should make a plan to determine how you're going to accomplish each task. How do you go about making a plan. First, you need to see where you are spending your time at the present (see figure 1-3). Chart the approximate number of hours you spend:

- getting ready for, going to and spending time in class
- getting ready for, going to, and working at your job
- with your family or friends (this includes time on the telephone)
- doing housework, preparing meals, doing laundry, taking care of the kids
- doing recreational activities, like working out, watching TV, or listening to your music

FIGURE 1-3 WEEK PLANNER

You should probably have a pretty good idea about what time is available to study and sleep. I know you're thinking, "No problem. If I just give up sleeping there will be plenty of time to study." However, it's not as bad as you think. The twenty-four hour week can be broken into many different lengths of time. There will be 15 minutes here and a half-hour there that will add up. Actually it is better to have some shorter study periods instead of only a few large blocks of time. Figure 1-4 on page 13 shows a sample of a time management plan that incorporates a twenty-four hour study plan while working full-time.

The plan in figure one uses some study techniques that are not ordinarily used. Because time is at such a premium for most community college students some short cuts are necessary. The following are suggestions that might help when you create your study plan.

- Tape record lectures from your professor, then when traveling to and from work or school, review the lecture by using your tape recorder.
- Tape record your lecture notes by reading them out loud. This can help in a number of ways. First, you'll have found an alternative method of studying by using the same techniques as discussed above; second, it will help you remember and learn the lecture material by both hearing it and seeing it; third, when you read material out loud there is a tendency to reorganize it and to put it in your own words. This also aids in the learning process.
- Carry note cards and study between classes. If you keep a set of note cards in an outer pocket of a book bag or in a shirt or coat pocket, they will be readily available to look over on short notice, such as when you are waiting in a line.

WHERE SHOULD I STUDY?

One of the first things we tell students when asked about finding a place to study is to make sure they connect the place where they study to a place where they can do serious work. For some students this means that they must do the bulk of their studying in a place like the library or in a place outside the home. This sometimes may be accomplished by scheduling classes so there are several hours available between classes. This will allow the student to use the college library. For most people, the college library is an excellent place to study. It is not only a conducive place to learn, it is also a place where many of the academic resources are located. Reference materials, computers, etc. can be found there. However, many students don't have the luxury of spending fifteen to twenty extra hours a week away from home. Therefore, for most students, studying at home is the only option. However, when a student does find time to study in the library, they should take the opportunity.

FIGURE 1-4   24 HOUR WEEKLY STUDY PLAN

	MON	TUE	WED	THU	FRI	SAT	SUN
6:00-700	wup	wup	wup	wup	wup	wup	wup
7:00-7:30	sic	sic	sic	sic	sic	frt	frt
7:30-9:00	w	w	w	w	w	st	st
9:00-10:00	w	w	w	w	w	sic	st
10:00-11:00	w	w	w	w	w	sic	frt
11:00-12:00	w	w	w	w	w	sic	st
12:00-1:00	w	w	w	w	w	frt	st
1:00-2:00	w	w	w	w	w	frt	frt
2:00-3:30	w	w	w	w	w	st	st
3:30-4:00	sic	sic	sic	sic	sic	frt	frt
4:00-5:00	frt	frt	frt	frt	frt	frt	frt
5:00-7:00	frt	frt	frt	frt	frt	frt	frt
7:00-8:00	sic	st	sic	st	sic	st	st
8:00-9:30	sic	st	sic	st	sic	frt	frt
9:30-10:00	sic	frt	sic	frt	sic	frt	frt
10:00-11:00	st	st	st	st	st	frt	frt

wup = wake up   w = work   sic = study in car
frt = free time   st = study time   sic = study in class

Studying at home can present some problems. There are usually other people around--husbands, wives, children or roommates. All of these people can present a distraction, not allowing you to concentrate and to work seriously. When trying to overcome problems with finding a place to study. The following are a number of options you may consider:

1. Make arrangements with your spouse or roommate. You may want to set aside particular times when you will be studying and you should not be disturbed.

2. You may find time at home when there is no one around. It may be late at night or early in the morning, but you will be able to study and concentrate without much disruption.

3. Children need a lot of time and energy, especially young children. Unless excellent child care is available and affordable, it would probably be best to begin your college career slowly. Also, try to plan "child time" into your schedule; when you devote your full attention to your children, they are more likely to play on their own and go to sleep easily and understand your need for study time.

4. When choosing a place to study, you need to find a place where you believe work can be done. Your bed is probably not going to be a place where you can concentrate for long periods of time. Sitting in front of the TV (whether it's on or off) is also not one of those places most people can concentrate. You need a place where psychologically, you feel ready to put in serious time. When it is impossible to have a totally quiet place, some people find that playing soft music reduces the background noise (it will probably help to wear headphones). Another thing to consider when choosing a place to study is to make sure that you have all your equipment with you when you begin to study, like notebooks, pens, a stapler, a highlighter, index cards, a dictionary and a thesaurus. If you don't have a desk that is convenient, but you can use a kitchen or dining room table, be sure to keep a book bag or even a cardboard box close by to

hold your equipment. Try to find a place with good lighting, a flat surface and a comfortable (but not too comfortable) chair.

Studying, as much as anything, is a state of mind. So you need to try your hardest not to let external things distract you from your work.

MAKE YOUR STUDY PLAN WORK

Since you have already mapped out a schedule for yourself and have secured a workable place for your study, how should you go about the task of actually getting under way? One of the first things you should do is to make some judgments about the difficulty of your courses. Some classes, because of the professor or the success you have had in the past with the type of material, will demand a greater amount of your time and energy. For example, if you are taking a science class you will probably have two sets of material to be studying, the material from the lectures and the more practical information from the labs. Courses like lab sciences usually require more time. So when you start studying, make sure that you budget extra time for this type of course.

Another thing to think about when planning your study time is which course you will study first. The tendency for most people is to study the areas you like or are more capable in first. This leaves your more difficult material for when you are tired or running out of time. So, the courses that you most need to put your energy into get the least amount of attention. The answer to this, of course, is to work on your least favorite or most difficult subjects first. If you get into the habit of tackling tough material early, you will find that your chances of getting everything completed according to your plan will be a great deal more likely.

A third thing to think about when planning your study strategies is the time of day you are at your most productive. Again, you should make judgments about when you are the most alert and when you do your best work. Some people are morning people, some work better at night. You need to pick your best time for studying and schedule your most difficult courses into this slot. This will allow you to give your best effort to the classes that are going to be the most difficult for you.

Plan the Entire Semester

As has been mentioned earlier, the amount and the concentration of your study time will fluctuate throughout the semester. There will be several exams or papers due all in the same week. Look ahead. Don't get caught having to cram a lot of material into a short period of time. If you have a major paper due on the twelfth or the thirteenth week of the semester, don't wait until a week before it's due to get started. For a long term project, budget small bits of your study time each day or every couple of days from the beginning of the semester. This might even allow you to turn your paper in before it's due. Most professors appreciate getting early papers, so it can't hurt your grade.

IS YOUR PLAN WORKING?

The first plan you make as a new college student won't be the last plan. As a matter of fact, successful students evaluate and re-evaluate their plans several times a semester. The best way to decide if your plan is working is by asking the following questions:

- Am I consistently following the time schedule that I wrote down?
- Am I practicing the study techniques that I thought would be helpful? (i.e., studying hard subjects first, studying for several short periods, etc.)
- Am I using all the "assistance departments" available on or off campus? (i.e., computer labs, writing lab, math lab, library resources etc.)
- Am I working on papers or projects that are due later in the semester?
- Am I getting the results that I expected?

If you are satisfied that you are on the right track, keep following the schedule you have. If you are not getting the results you want, check to see if you can make some adjustments in your plan.

EXERCISES CHAPTER ONE

Exercise 1-1 a & b FINDING YOUR GPA

Instructions: Find the GPA's for these students using the quality point formula given in your text.

Ex. 1-1a

SUBJECT	CREDITS	GRADE	GRADE EQUIV.	TOTAL
Spanish	3	A	_____	_____
Algebra	3	C	_____	_____
Art	3	B	_____	_____
Psych	3	B	_____	_____
Biology	4	C	_____	_____

Sums _____

_____ =GPA

Ex. 1-1b

SUBJECT	CREDITS	GRADE	GRADE EQUIV.	TOTAL
Health	1	A	_____	_____
Calculus	3	B	_____	_____
Literature	3	A	_____	_____
Physics	4	C	_____	_____
Law	3	A	_____	_____

Sums _____

_____ =GPA

Exercise 1-2 RESOURCES ON CAMPUS

Instructions: Give a brief description of what services are provided by the following areas and state their location on campus.

1. Tutoring:_____

   _____

   _____

   Building: _____ Rm: _____

2. Computer lab:_____

   _____

   _____

   Building: _____ Rm: _____

3. Math or writing lab: _____

   _____

   _____

   Building: _____ Rm: _____

4. Library_:_____

   _____

   Building: _____ Rm: _____

5. Branch campuses: Town of location; _____

   Street of branch campus; _____

   Three degrees available at branch campus;

   a. _____

   b. _____

   c. _____

Exercise 1-3b

Instructions: List and describe four ways a student can begin to handle stress.

1. _____

   _____

   _____

   _____

2. _____

   _____

   _____

   _____

3. _____

   _____

   _____

   _____

4. _____

   _____

   _____

   _____

Exercise 1-4

Instructions: In the grid below create your best study schedule. Remember to be creative, be realistic. You need time for relaxation and to be with the people your care for.

Exercise 1.4   WEEK PLANNER

	MON	TUE	WED	THU	FRI	SAT	SUN
6—7							
7—8							
8—9							
9—10							
10—11							
11—12							
12—1							
1—2							
2—3							
3—4							
4—5							
5—6							
6—7							
7—8							
8—9							
9—10							
10—11							
11—12							

Exercise 1-5

Instructions: Discuss how the following statements can be an advantage or a disadvantage to you when you are trying to do serious studying.

1. Using the library to study: _____

_____

_____

_____

_____

2. Tape recording lectures: _____

_____

_____

_____

_____

3. Reading textbooks in bed: _____

_____

_____

_____

_____

4. Changing your place of study everyday: _____

_____

_____

_____

5. Talk to your friends on the phone while you study:_____

_____

_____

_____

Reading a College Textbook

Introduction In this chapter you will learn the best way to read a college textbook. You will read and practice techniques that will increase your reading speed as well as your comprehension. Also, through exercises and examples, you will learn how to make your textbook an effective learning tool.

Goals After you have completed the work in this chapter, you will:

- Use your textbook as an important learning tool, with specific sections and unique features.
- Acknowledge the textbook as an important resource for success in the course
- Enjoy increased reading comprehension and speed
- Accept how logic and reasoning enhance the thinking process.

Activities/Tasks This section describes the steps you need to take in order to complete the activities in the chapter. You should check off each activity/task as you complete it.

1. Survey the textbook for general resources (Table of Content, Glossary, Subject Index)_____
2. Survey two chapters of the textbook for chapter objectives, vocabulary, summary test questions_____
3. Locate a novel (or other non-textbook) and survey it for the above features (ACTION)_____
4. Highlight two pages of the textbook for the important information, such as topic sentences, important definitions, important examples_____
5. Underline and use abbreviations on two pages of textbook to show important points in the text.
6. Read and complete the critical thinking assignment_____
7. Answer or add at least one general knowledge question._____

Learning Objectives	These are the assignments you need to complete and show or submit to your instructor.

1. Participate in a small group discussion about how and where to survey a text and the differences between a textbook and a novel or other kind of book.
2. Hand into the instructor an exercise on how to effectively "mark" your textbook.
3. Submit to the instructor a sample of a well highlighted textbook page.
4. Participate in a small group discussion on the Do's & Don'ts of textbook reading.
5. Write and submit an essay on critical thinking incorporating the summary of an article.
6. Contribute to the general knowledge fund.

Chapter Two: How to Read a College Textbook

What problems can reading a textbook pose? You open the book to page one and you begin to read. When the chapter ends, you stop. Sounds pretty simple, except for most students it does not work very well. Many students really don't remember much about what they read. Usually it is not because they are poor readers; it is because they have never learned how to read a textbook. Textbook reading is different from reading novels; because the chapters and the text are organized differently. Textbook reading is more like reading short essays on a specific topic. Just like in a good essay, the ideas connect but they can also be put in a different order. The worst way to read a textbook, especially one designed for college, is to read it like a novel. In a novel, there isn't necessarily a beginning, a middle and an end. As a matter of fact, much of a textbook's information can be presented in any number of different ways. A chapter near the end could easily be placed in the beginning or in the middle of the book. We're not saying that there are topics that couldn't be arranged sequentially; a child psychology textbook makes more sense if you begin at conception and progress through the child's life chronologically. We are saying that there is a great deal of latitude when constructing the order of a textbook. When a textbook writer publishes a book, the order of information is generally his or her choice.

How does this affect the textbook reader? In some ways it helps. It gives the reader a chance to organize the material that they are reading into something they can understand. They can pick out the material that they understand in the chapter, work on it until they learn it, and then go onto the rest of the chapter.

Textbook reading is a skill that can be acquired; however, you have to understand what goals you are trying to achieve. Textbooks range in depth and complexity and you can not read each one in the same way. With some textbooks you have to read very slowly to get the most out of them. Other texts, you will be able to read much more easily. However, no matter how difficult the textbook there are methods to increase your reading efficiency.

YOU CAN LEARN A METHOD FOR READING COLLEGE TEXTBOOKS—SQ3R

There are many techniques that can be used to read textbooks. The method that we have found to be the easiest to understand and the most useful to a beginning community college student is called the SQ3R method.

This is not a new method; however, it is one of the best, because this approach employs all the basic principles for reading and remembering new information. Each section of SQ3R helps prepare the student to read a college textbook.

The SQ3R stands for:

S = Survey
Q = Question
R = Read
R = Recite
R = Review

SQRRR: SURVEY

To survey a textbook means to look over the book to see how it is organized and see what types of information are included. Usually, examining a textbook is broken into two surveys. The first survey gives a general analysis of the text. The reader looks to see how many chapters there are in the textbook and see how the information is organized. The second survey focuses on the individual chapters to see if there are additional sections that might help with understanding the text.

The General Survey

When doing a general survey of a textbook, you should realize that most textbooks provide a great deal of the general information in their Table of Contents. The Table of Contents is a listing of all the important topics that are contained in the textbook. It will usually give a chapter-by-chapter description, highlighting the main sub-headings within each chapter and describing important topics. (See Figure 2-1)

The general survey should also involve checking if there are additional sections of the text which are designed to help the reader know more about the technical aspects of the text like the vocabulary or the authors that are quoted. These sections are usually in the back of the book and can include:

- A glossary is like a dictionary for the textbook. It will include definitions of much of the special vocabulary used in the text.
- An index, a list the pages where specific information can be found. There may be several kinds of indexes, in most texts, at least a subject index and an author index is included. The subject index lists the pages where vocabulary terms, theories, ideas and concepts are located within the textbook chapter. The author index, gives the pages where a certain author has been mentioned or referenced in the text. These are usually presented in alphabetical order.
- An appendix contains information the writer thinks is important but not crucial enough or too technical or detailed to include in the chapters of the textbook. Information that might be included in the appendix could be a chart about the metric system in a math textbook or the full text of the Declaration of Independence in an American History textbook.
- The reference section is an alphabetical listing of authors and their works cited throughout the textbook and the pages where the citation may be found.

FIGURE 2-1   **An Example of the First Chapter in A Table of Contents**

CONTENTS

PART ONE

Study Skills

The Chapter Survey

The second step in surveying a textbook is to look over the individual chapters. Most texts at the beginning and the end of each chapter have sections that are designed to help the reader understand the material better. For example, in the beginning of a chapter in many textbooks you will find a listing of the subheadings or the major sections within the chapter. This technique is designed to prepare the student for what the author believes are the important topics within the chapter. Other texts may start off by giving a list of objectives or questions about the material within the chapter. The reason the author uses this technique is to start the reader thinking about and questioning what material is important in the chapter. Each of these sections are put in so the reader can look for specific information; looking for specific information while you read will help with reading comprehension.

Another way a textbook writer tries to help the reader is by adding helpful sections to the end of a chapter. Many times a textbook chapter will include a summary of the chapter or will list main points about the material within the chapter. By doing this, the author is giving the reader an outline of the important information in the chapter. Most textbook chapters will also give lists of important vocabulary used in the chapter.

Again, all these sections are designed to help the reader understand the chapter better. Therefore, the best way to read a textbook chapter is to look at the section with the author's questions or objectives in the beginning and then skip to the end of the chapter and read the summary and examine the new vocabulary. These tips will help with reading comprehension and will focus your attention on specific facts and ideas included in that chapter. When a person is looking for ideas as they read they are likely to find them. Survey each chapter of a new textbook. It will help the reader increase their understanding of what they read.

S**QRRR**: QUESTION

What is the purpose of questioning, while reading a college textbook? The purpose is to focus the student's attention on the main points of a chapter. A textbook author attempts to do the same thing by providing objectives or by listing main points in the beginnings of each chapter. The important element when you use the questioning technique, is to become involved with the information that the author is trying to convey. When you read a textbook you need to be involved, you need to become an active reader.

How many times have you begun to read a chapter in your textbook and ten or fifteen minutes into your reading you stop. You ask yourself, "What have I just read?", and realize you don't have a clue. You have just spent a significant portion of your study time and you know nothing! You thought you were reading, but you were actually just wasting time. Many times, students think that if they move their eyes across a page of text, the information is going to jump into their brains. It doesn't work that way.

To learn, you have to become an active reader and use the questioning process to become involved with the information in the text. If you begin by asking questions about the material, you will be looking for answers within the text. When you focus your attention on what is happening in the text, you will begin to understand how the parts of the book fit together and how the facts that you are reading have meaning.

The best way to start the questioning process is to look at the individual chapters and figure out what questions, concerning the subheadings from each chapter are the most important when trying to understand the main ideas. For example, as you are reading this text you would ask, "How will surveying a textbook help me be a better textbook reader?" or "Why does questioning help me to better focus my reading." In each case, you will be looking for specific information within the material that will help you understand the text. As you become more practiced at asking questions about the information in the text you will begin to get greater detail and more complexity in your questions. (See Figure 2-2)

FIGURE 2-2   **Questions that help you to understand**

1. What is a glossary and what value does the glossary have when reading a
    textbook?

2. Name two types of indexes and state how they help you understand the text?

3. The Appendix contains what type of information?

4. What is a reference section and how does it help the reader to understand the text book better?

SQRRR: READING

To read a textbook means to understand facts, ideas, concepts and theories presented in written form. This sounds like something that would be difficult to do, but it is not as hard as you may think. The great thing about reading is that when you have a textbook in front of you, you can go back at any time and read it again. There is no way to misplace the meaning of the author. It is permanent in the text and can be found with time and perseverance.

Reading textbooks can also be very difficult—the author isn't with you to explain or describe what he or she means. If you do not understand a passage or an idea, if the facts don't relate or the theories don't seem to have any practical value, then reading a textbook becomes a chore.

So what can you do? Since you are going to have to be an efficient textbook reader or have a great deal of difficulty in reaching your goal of graduating from college. You may try to follow the suggestions listed below.

How do you avoid problems in textbook reading?

1. You have to be patient. You may have to struggle to get focused on the material. You may not be able to sit down and read a textbook for an hour or an hour and a half at first. You may have to read in short bursts of fifteen or twenty minutes at a time, but with focus and attention you will be able to build up your speed. Reading is like weight lifting—you don't start lifting 500 pounds on day one, you start with 10 pound weights and build. It takes time and effort, but if you give your self a chance you'll succeed.
2. You need to be active in your reading, as was discussed in the Questioning Section of this chapter. When you have a purpose in your reading, you're more likely to understand what has been written.
3. You can be active in your reading by trying to learn things from the most important to the least important. Try to remember the main topics before you try to memorize the smallest details. For example, know what SQ3R stands for before learning how the glossary of the textbook works.

4. You need to be inquisitive. You have to search for new things to learn. This may sound pretentious, but reading is the gateway to success. Even though it may seem boring at first or at times the text doesn't make sense, the more you practice the easier textbook reading becomes.

Another important way to focus your attention on the main points is by using notes, checks and symbols or highlighting to mark important information in your textbook (this is called marking a textbook). Marking can take several different forms. The most popular way of marking is by using highlighters. Highlighters come in many different colors and widths. Their main purpose is to indicate to the student what facts, ideas and examples are important and what information can be skimmed over.

Two problems that arise when using highlighters is how much and where to highlight. The most common error in highlighting is coloring too much of the page. We have looked through hundreds of texts and seen 70%—80% of each page highlighted. This defeats the purpose of the marking. What you want is to be able to open up the book, turn to a page and examine it and see if you know or if you don't know the material. You want to do this by simply scanning the main ideas and important examples. If most of the page is highlighted you end up reading the whole page over again to see if you know the information. (See Figure 2—3 Too much highlighting)

FIGURE 2-3 **Too much highlighting**

Question

What is the purpose of questioning, when reading a college textbook? The purpose is to focus the student's attention to the main points of a chapter. A textbook author attempts to do the same things by providing chapter objectives or by listing main points in their books. The main point of questioning, is to become involved with the information that the author is trying to convey. When you read a textbook you need to be involved, you need to become an active reader.

How many times have you begun to read a chapter in your textbook and ten or fifteen minutes into your reading you stop. You ask yourself, "What have I just read?", and realize you don't have a clue. You have just spent a significant portion of your study time and you know nothing. You thought you were reading, but you were actually just wasting time. Many times, students think that if they move their eyes across a page of text, the information is going to jump into their brains. It doesn't work that way.

To learn, you have to become an active reader and use the questioning process to become involved with the information in the text. If you begin by asking questions about the material, you will be looking for answers within the text. When you focus your attention to what is happening in the text you will begin to understand the purpose of the book.

The best way to start the questioning process is to figure out what questions, concerning the main ideas or subheadings from each chapter, are the most important when trying to understand the main ideas of the chapter. For example, as you are reading this text you would ask, "How will surveying a textbook help me be a better textbook reader?" or "Why does questioning help me to better focus my reading." In each case as you continue your reading you will be looking for specific information within the material. As you become more practiced at asking questions about the information in the text you will begin to get greater detail and more complexity in your questioning.

On the other side of the coin, sometimes students don't highlight enough. They may mark single vocabulary words or random facts, which does not allow the student to make judgments about what they know or what they don't know about what is being presented on that page. (See Figure 2-4 Too little highlighting)

FIGURE 2-4   Too little highlighting

Question

What is the purpose of questioning, when reading a college textbook? The purpose is to focus the student's attention to the main points of a chapter. A textbook author attempts to do the same things by providing chapter objectives or by listing main points in their books. The main point of questioning, is to become involved with the information that the author is trying to convey. When you read a textbook you need to be involved, you need to become an active reader.

How many times have you begun to read a chapter in your textbook and ten or fifteen minutes into your reading you stop. You ask yourself, "What have I just read?", and realize you don't have a clue. You have just spent a significant portion of your study time and you know nothing. You thought you were reading, but you were actually just wasting time. Many times, students think that if they move their eyes across a page of text, the information is going to jump into their brains. It doesn't work that way.

To learn, you have to become an active reader and use the *questioning* process to become involved with the information in the text. If you begin by asking questions about the material, you will be looking for answers within the text. When you focus your attention to what is happening in the text you will begin to understand the purpose of the book.

The best way to start the *questioning* process is to figure out what *questions*, concerning the main ideas or subheadings from each chapter, are the most important when trying to understand the main ideas of the chapter. For example, as you are reading this text you would ask, "How will surveying a textbook help me be a better textbook reader?" or "Why does questioning help me to better focus my reading." In each case as you continue your reading you will be looking for specific information within the material. As you become more practiced at asking questions about the information in the text you will begin to get greater detail and more complexity in your questions.

The correct amount of highlighting can differ with the type of textbook being used, but as a general rule you will probably be able to cover the main topics and get a good idea about what is on a particular page when you are highlighting between 25 and 35 percent of a page. This will allow you to skim over material and still have a good idea of what is included. (see Figure 2—5 The correct amount of highlighting)

FIGURE 2-5   **The correct amount of highlighting**

Question

What is the purpose of questioning, when reading a college textbook? The purpose is to focus the student's attention to the main points of a chapter. A textbook author attempts to do the same things by providing chapter objectives or by listing main points in their books. The main point of questioning, is to become involved with the information that the author is trying to convey. When you read a textbook you need to be involved, you need to become an active reader.

How many times have you begun to read a chapter in your textbook and ten or fifteen minutes into your reading you stop. You ask yourself, "What have I just read?", and realize you don't have a clue. You have just spent a significant portion of your study time and you know nothing. You thought you were reading, but you were actually just wasting time. Many times, students think that if they move their eyes across a page of text, the information is going to jump into their brains, It doesn't work that way.

To learn, you have to become an active reader and use the questioning process to become involved with the information in the text. If you begin by asking questions about the material, you will be looking for answers within the text. When you focus your attention to what is happening in the text you will begin to understand the purpose of the book.

The best way to start the questioning process is to figure out what questions, concerning the main ideas or subheadings from each chapter are the most important when trying to understand the main ideas of the chapter. For example, as you are reading this text you would ask, "How will surveying a textbook help me be a better textbook reader?" or "Why does questioning help me to better focus my reading." In each case as you continue your reading you will be looking for specific information within the material. As you become more practiced at asking questions about the information in the text you will begin to get greater detail and more complexity in your questions.

Another method that may be helpful when using highlighters is to assign different colors to various types of information. For example, you may want to use a yellow high lighter for facts like names, dates and ideas then use a blue highlighter to show examples or illustrations of these ideas This type of color coding will allow you to have some idea about what type of material is contained on each page when you're beginning your review. This also focuses your attention so that when you are looking for a particular thing within the text you can find it.

This again is another technique that can increase your reading comprehension.

You may also want to try underlining as a way to focus your attention to important information. Underlining can be used instead of highlighting or it can be used in conjunction with highlighting. Sometimes you can underline to prioritized your highlighted material by using single lines to show that a sentence or a phrase is of even more importance.

Another helpful marking technique is to write abbreviations, numbers and symbols in the margins and text of your book. You can do this to indicate the importance or the type of material that is contained in the text. This technique is similar to the one we will discuss during the, *Taking Notes from Lecture*, section of this book. First, you can use abbreviations to show the type of material contained in the text, such as **def.** to indicate that there is a definition or to use **ex.** to show an example.

Second, you may use numbers to illustrate a series of facts or ideas enclose in the text. For example, if the text states that there were five causes to the Civil War, you would number each of these five causes in the text itself. Last, you might use the symbol '**?**' in the margin of your textbook to show that you were not clear about some fact or idea contained in a passage.(See figure 2-6 Use underlining and abbreviations to show what is important points in the text)

Marking, whether using a highlighter or underlining keeps the reader active in the reading process. It also brings out important information when it is time to study for a test. So, use some marking techniques and help yourself become a more effective reader.

FIGURE 2-6   **Use underlining and abbreviations to show important points in the text**

The general survey will also involve checking if there are additional sections of the text which are designed to help the reader. These sections are usually in the back of the book and can include:

def →A glossary is like a dictionary for the textbook. It will include definitions of much of the special vocabulary used in the text.

ex→ There may be several kinds of *indexes*, in most texts, at least a subject index and an author index is included. The subject index lists the pages where vocabulary terms, theories, ideas and concepts are located within the textbook chapter. The author index, gives the pages where a certain author has been mentioned or referenced in the text. These are usually presented in alphabetical order.

? → The *appendix* contains information the writer thinks is important but not crucial enough to include in the chapters of the textbook. Information that might be included in the appendix could be a chart about the metric system in a math textbook or the full text of the Declaration of Independence in an American History textbook.

imp → The *reference* section is an alphabetical listing of authors and their works cited. The reference section indicates the pages where authors and the works cited can be found throughout the textbook.

An additional way to survey a textbook is to <u>look over the individual chapters</u>. Most texts at the <u>beginning</u> and the <u>end of each chapter</u> have sections that are designed to help the reader understand the material better. For <u>example</u>, in the <u>beginning of a chapter</u> in many textbooks you will find a listing of the <u>subheadings</u> or the major sections within the chapter. This technique is designed to prepare the student for what the author believes are the important topic within the chapter. Other texts may begin by giving a <u>list of objectives</u> or <u>questions</u> about the material within the chapter. The reason the author uses this technique is to help the reader start thinking about and <u>questioning what material is important in the chapter</u>. Each of these sections is available so the reader can look for specific information (looking for specific information while you read will help with reading comprehension).

Another way a textbook writer tries to help the reader is by adding helpful sections to the <u>end of a chapter</u>. Many times a textbook chapter will include a <u>summary of the chapter</u> or will list <u>main points</u> about the material within the chapter. By doing this the author is actually giving the reader an outline of the important information in the chapter. Most textbook chapters will also, give lists of <u>important vocabulary</u> used in the chapter. Again, all these sections are designed to help the reader understand the chapter better.

Therefore, the best way to read a textbook chapter is to look at the section with the author's questions or objectives in the beginning and then skip to the end of the chapter and read the summary and examine the new vocabulary. This will <u>help with reading comprehension</u> and will focus the reader's <u>attention to specific facts</u> and ideas included in that chapter. When a person is looking for ideas as they read they are likely to find them. Survey each chapter of a new textbook. It will help the reader increase their understanding of what they read.

MARKING DIFFERENT TYPES OF TEXTBOOKS

You should also be aware that different types of textbooks should be marked with different emphasis. Certain types of textbooks like science books, math books, novels, plays or literature texts may need a special type of marking. For example, with science and math texts formulas or examples of problems may be the most important information in the book. The student needs to be able to show that this is the material that they need to learn. Formulas or examples of problems should be circled or squared as shown in **(Figure 2—7).** In addition, the formulas or examples should be prioritized, in terms of importance. One way to prioritize this type of material is by using the star system:

one *   = important
two **   = very important
three ***   = must know

FIGURE 2-7   **Marking a statistics textbook**

TABLE 1—1 Expected frequencies

	REPUBLICAN	DEMOCRAT	TOTALS
Male	39	61	100
Female	51	20	71
Total	90	81	171

The proportion of republicans in the sample is 90/171. There are 100 men in the sample and 90/1 71 of 100 is 53.

$$(90/171(100) = 53)$$

Similarly, the expected frequency of republicans among the women is 26.5.

$$(90/171(50) = 26.5)$$

In other types of books like novels, plays or literature texts, marking may also be different. Unlike reading a social science or humanities textbook, you are not necessarily looking for the most important factual information in literature books. The emphasis in these types of books is generally aimed at finding themes or recognizing characters and their traits. When marking this kind of book, the student needs to be clear about the types of things they want to emphasize so that they don't confuse the material even further.

SQRRr: RECITE

The second R in SQ3R is RECITE. Reciting means to speak out loud to yourself or to another person. The reason for reciting or recitation is two-fold. First, when a person both sees and hears information, they are more likely to remember that material than if they just heard or read it. However, you want to limit the amount of material you had read out loud because it does slow you down and you want to concentrate on the important information in the chapter. So the reciting part should begin after you have highlighted and marked your book. Once you have finished a section of your text (for example a major subheading) you may want to state out loud the important points within that section (probably the items you highlighted or underlined). Try to make sense of what you have just read and see if you can recall some of the major details. If you can't then you should go back and read the material again.

A second way recitation can help you learn the material is that when you talk about the important information you will probably put it in to your own words. Any time you can put new ideas into your own words you are well on your way to learning it.

Another hint about recitation, it does help to recite to another person. They can tell you if what you're saying makes sense. They can also help with questions about the new information, which again helps in the learning process.

SQRR: REVIEW

The last R in SQ3R is REVIEW. The process of reviewing material presented from the text of the book is the only way to really learn the information. You need to become very familiar with the information before you can really use it. Some students use the old cram method to try learning new material. This is just rote memorization and is the least effective way to learn new information. The most efficient way to learn new information is to practice it on a consistent basis, if you were going to study for a three chapter exam the best way to do it would be to:

> Survey the chapters, check vocabulary, read the summary, read that first chapter, and go back.
> Mark that chapter for the most important parts.
> Recite chapter one, find out what you know and what you don't know.
> Create flash cards (see Ch. 3), and concept maps (see Ch. 5), as study tools.
> When you have finished Chapter one, go on and use the same process with Chapter two.
> When you finish with chapter 'two', go back and review chapter one. You follow these same procedures until you have completed all three chapters.

You will not have enough time to do this type of studying if you wait until the last minute. You must start the first day you know what material is going to be included on the test. When the exam comes around, you will be prepared. You will have time to review and look over the material. No more late night cramming, a lot less anxiety and probably better grades.

INCREASE YOUR READING SPEED WHILE INCREASING YOUR COMPREHENSION

It makes no sense to increase the speed at which you read if you don't understand the material afterward. SQ3R provided you with a way to approach a new textbook. It gives some ideas about what you can do before and during the time you are reading a text to increase your understanding of the book. Here are some additional techniques you can use to not only increase your understanding but actually increase your overall reading speed.

Probably the best way to increase your reading speed is to just try to read faster. This may seem like a very simple answer, but the muscles it takes to read need to be conditioned just like any other muscle in your body. Your eyes need practice to move faster and focus longer on the textbook page. Your attention needs to be concentrated on a specific task for longer periods of time. All of these things take time and patience. In the beginning, it might be difficult to try to read faster especially if you are trying to do it for a long period of time. The best way to begin to read faster is to concentrate on passages for short bursts. Try to read half or even one quarter of a page as quickly as you can and then slow down for the same amount of a page. Continue this throughout your reading period. This can also help you to understand the material better. When your attention is focused on a particular task, you are more likely to understand.

A second way to increase reading speed is to eliminate skipping over words in the text. One of the biggest problems that occurs when reading a textbook is that your eyes don't move smoothly over the page. Your vision actually bounces from one word or group of words to the next. So, many people continually lose their place and read lines they have already gone over. This will of course slow you down and disrupt a smooth reading pace. One way to help with this problem is to use an index card to help you follow each line.

Take a 5 by 8 index card and cut out a window that will display just one line of text at a time. This blocks out the line above and the line below and allows you to focus on what you are reading. You pull the card down as you complete reading each line. This will prevent your eyes from skipping around on the page. This method should only be used to get you started. You will be able to read much faster once you have trained your reading eyes.

A third way to increase your reading speed is to know when to skim or scan certain passages within the text. Not all the material in each chapter needs to be read thoroughly. There are passages and paragraphs that don't contain information you need. These passages may be transition paragraphs used by the writer to move from one idea to the next, or they may be passages that sum up or repeat material already discussed. If you can skim these passages then you can also increase your speed.

The technique for scanning and skimming is really just the process of identifying the main idea within each paragraph. You can do this by finding the topic sentence for a particular paragraph. The topic sentence contains the main idea and identifies what the rest of the paragraph is going to be about. Once you find the topic sentence, you can make a decision whether you should read the rest of the paragraph or not.

Where can you find the topic sentence? In most textbooks the vast majority of paragraphs have their first sentence as the topic sentence. Therefore, most of the time all you have to do is read the first sentence of each paragraph to find the main idea and make your decision. If, you can't find the topic sentence in the first line, then go to the last line of the paragraph. This is the second most likely place to find the topic sentence. Finding the topic sentence will also help you increase your reading comprehension, because it will focus your attention on the most important material on that page.

TAKING NOTES FROM THE TEXTBOOK

Taking notes from your textbook can be a task that you are not used to doing. The first problem is that there is so much information on each page. How do you know what is important and what is not important? The best way to start is see what the author of the text thinks is important. In the Survey section of this chapter, we discussed how many authors of textbooks provide outlines of the chapter or list the main points of the chapter. Sometimes they will give a list of questions that the reader should be able to answer after reading the chapter. These are all good places to begin. They are usually general in nature and deal with broad topics throughout the chapter. After reading a paragraph or a section, see if you are able to pick out the main points and answer the question posed by the author. Try to pick out the main points, and answer the questions that are being asked. If you can't, these are good topics to take notes on. These are areas that will need additional study. It is also a good idea to match the notes you are taking down from your text to the notes you took from the lecture. You will begin to start making judgment about what is important and what is not important.

EXERCISE CHAPTER TWO

Exercise 2—1 The five steps to Better textbook reading

Instructions: List the term for the acronym **SQ3R** and give a brief definition of each word.

S _____

_____

Q _____

_____

R _____

_____

R _____

_____

R _____

_____

Exercise 2—2 The General Survey

Instructions: Name four of the major areas that should be checked during a general survey.

1. _____
2. _____
3. _____
4. _____

Exercise 2—3 The chapter survey

Instructions: Explain how a chapter survey can help you understand the text-book better when considering these topics:

1. Chapter sub-headings _____

_____

_____

2. Objectives or questions _____

_____

_____

3. A summary or main points _____

_____

_____

4. Vocabulary Terms _____

_____

_____

Exercise 2—7 Reasons to recite when you read a textbook

Instructions: Give three reasons why reciting helps a textbook reader remember the material better.

1. _____

   _____

   _____

2. _____

   _____

   _____

3. _____

   _____

   _____

Exercise 2—8 Reviewing a textbook for an exam

Instructions: Explain how you might for an exam on chapters 1, 2, & 3 using the principles outlined in the review section of this chapter.

_____

_____

_____

_____

_____

_____

_____

Exercise 2—9 Increase your reading speed

Instructions:

1. Using a textbook from another class, pick three full pages of text and time yourself. You want be sure that you can describe the major topic within those three pages after you have finished reading.

2. Using the same textbook, choose another three pages of text and time your self. However, this time use the suggestions from the section of this chapter on how to increase your reading speed. Pay special attention to: a) trying to read faster; b) reading to find the topic sentence; c) reading from major information to specific details.

3. Check to see if there is any improvement over both the speed at which you read and the amount of information you remembered.

Taking Notes From Lecture

| Introduction | In this chapter, you will learn how to take better notes from lecture and you will practice techniques that will make your lecture notes more |

organized and complete. You will also learn, through readings and exercises, how to make your lecture notes a complementary tool to your textbook and other reading materials. You will continue to improve your critical thinking skills.

| Goals | After you have completed this chapter, you will: |

- Take high-quality notes from lecture in a stress-free manner.
- Enter the classroom confident that your time will be spent   in productive learning.
- Benefit from a set of complete and organized notes that will assist you at exam time.
- Extend your critical thinking and writing skills.

| Activities/Tasks | These are the steps you need to take in order to complete the activities in the chapter. You should check off as you complete activity or task. |

1. Read and take notes on the chapter._____
2. Select a class session and enter the classroom early. Sit in the first row (or as close as possible) in the center seat. (ACTION)_____
3. Prepare sheets of paper to use in two classes in the Cornell style of note taking._____
4. Use a previous set of lecture notes and put them into the Cornell style._____
5. Create five flash cards using the techniques in the textbook. Do this with a group._____
6. Write a study guide using the techniques in the textbook._____
7. Develop a list of abbreviations to use in notetaking._____
8. Complete the Critical Thinking exercises._____
9. Answer or add at least one question to the General Knowledge fund._____

| Learning Objectives | These are the assignments you need to complete and show or hand in to your instructor. |

1. Participate in a class discussion about how it felt to sit in the front of the class in the center seat. Were you there in mind and body?_____
2. Discuss in a small group how the 4 R's of note taking can be an advantage   getting the most out of taking notes from a lecture.
3. Use the Cornell style of note taking in at least two lecture sessions and show to your instructor._____
4. Hand-in your restructured notes from one previous lecture session._____
5. Create five flash cards, using the techniques from the textbook and vocabulary from a lecture session. Show to your instructor._____
6. Create a study guide using the format shown in the textbook and submit to your instructor._____
7. Share your list of a abbreviations that could be used when taking notes from a lecture._____
8. Complete the Critical Thinking exercises.
9. Contribute to the General Knowledge fund._____

Chapter Three: Taking Notes from Lectures

Notetaking may be the most frustrating task a college student faces. The professors always talk too fast and they skip around, so you never know what is coming next. Most of the time when you get home and you begin to review your notes, you realize you have absolutely no idea of what the professor was talking about in class. The problem is, in many of your college courses, the bulk of the information or the emphasis on what is important in your textbook, will come from the lecture. That makes having a complete and readable set of notes a must if you intend to do well in the class.

THE FOUR R'S OF NOTETAKING

1. You need to be ready physically and mentally for the job.

2. You need to record your notes as the professor gives the lecture.

3. You need to restructure your notes by filling in the blanks, clearing up confusing passages and relating the notes to other sources of information.

4. You need to review your notes and begin to learn them and put them into long-term memory. This is also the time you need to begin to prepare test-taking devices that will assist you in the study process for exams.

BE READY

Be There In Mind And Body

We tell our students that the most important aspect in taking notes is being in class both physically and mentally. Several students each semester come up to us and ask, "I don't seem to be doing well on your tests. Can you give me some advice about what I can change?" The first thing we do is check the attendance book. Nine times out of ten they have missed a significant amount of classes. If you don't attend, you can't take good notes. Some

students will respond, "But, I got the notes from a classmate." We answer, "Did these notes help you on the test?" The answer is obvious. You lose the flow of the class and you are unable to pick up the intent of your professor when you do not go to class every session. Taking notes can be difficult even when you are there every day, so why put yourself at an even greater disadvantage by not attending. Not only do you need to go to class, you need to get there on time. It is preferable to be in your seat at least five minutes before the lecture begins. This shows the professor you are interested in the class and avoids disrupting your classmates. Getting to class early also allows you to get your material ready for taking notes and allows you to get in the right frame of mind for listening and understanding.

Materials For Notetaking

Students should also be concerned with their choice of study tools when preparing to take notes. Many students start out using the wire-bound notebook that you find in most college bookstores, but in our experience the best and most efficient notebook is the three-ring binder. The three-ring binder allows the student to
- replace pages that they want to change or edit.
- place handouts or supplementary material in the appropriate areas of their notes.
- record additional notes from the textbook.
- keep their notes organized.

Another important tool you will need is the proper writing instrument. In today's market, you can easily purchase an inexpensive erasable pen that works well. Ordinary pens are OK but there is a tendency to scratch out material that is confusing or incomplete during the lecture. This makes the notes look messy and they become a less efficient study tool. Although this may seem like a small point, when your lecture notes look clean and organized, they are easier to read and easier to study from. There is also less of a tendency to copy over notes, which at times can be wasteful.

Other tools that are helpful when preparing to take notes from lectures are things like a ruler or a straight edge, which we will discuss during the **Recording** section of this chapter. Highlighters of two different colors, a dictionary or an electronic spell-checker for when you have time to correct spelling (usually right after the lecture or during a break) are also helpful. Maybe the most important aspect of having the right materials is that you have taken steps to be organized and ready to work at taking notes from lectures.

Knowing What Comes Next

A third way to be ready for taking notes from lecture is predicting what is going to be lectured about during the next session. There are a number of ways you can do this:

- **Read your textbook**—If the instructor is following a textbook, read ahead and have some idea of what the professor is going to talk about. This will help you to follow the lecture more closely and will allow you to better understand what is being discussed. If in your reading, you find vocabulary words that you're not sure of or if there are concepts you are finding difficult to understand, these may be good questions to ask your professor during the next lecture. You can't ask these questions if you're not ready and have not read ahead.

- **Read your notes from the previous lecture**—Most of the time there is a pattern. Many teachers will have a definite beginning and ending point in their lectures. At times, the professor will end their lectures by giving a synopsis of what they are going to talk about in their next class. Pay attention to these final remarks-- write them down. Find the topic in your text or in other supplementary material and you will be ready for your next lecture.

- **Check your syllabus**—Often a professor will have a tentative schedule of lecture material on his or her syllabus. Check off the items you have covered and you should have some idea of what will be covered next.

Anticipating lecture material and having some idea of what will be discussed next will help you to get a jump on the next lecture. When you know some of the vocabulary that will be used during the lecture, it will help you to focus your listening skills and give you a better quality of notes. You will begin to try to match up material you have read about or discussed earlier with the new material being lectured about that day. This will enable you to better understand the lecture and will allow you to take more complete notes.

A final area of consideration when preparing to take notes is where you sit in the classroom. If you get to class early, you should be able to get any seat you want. You should try to sit in the first few rows of the classroom. There are several reasons why this is important. If you sit in the front, the instructor will probably notice you and learn your name more quickly. This can help, especially if there is a grade for class participation. Once you are noticed, it gives you added motivation to be in class every session because the professor will also notice if you are not there. When you sit in the front you make a greater commitment to staying alert and taking the best notes possible. If you're prone to daydreaming or, worse, to falling asleep, you know that if you do, the instructor will notice you. This is not a good way of charming your professor into giving you an 'A'. Also, when you sit in front, you can hear better and see the board with greater clarity. Finally, there are fewer distractions in front of you, such as people talking or coughing or just not paying attention. Give it a try.

RECORD YOUR LECTURE NOTES

The second **R** in notetaking is recording. If you have followed the techniques just discussed, you will be prepared for taking notes. In this section of the chapter, we are going to discuss techniques for getting those notes down on paper or how to record your notes. The most effective style of taking notes from lectures was developed Professor Walter Pauk from Cornell University. The idea behind this style of notetaking is to allow the student to organize the lecture material and to annotate or embellish the information by using other sources such as the textbook.

The Cornell Style of Notetaking

Cornell style of notetaking requires ordinary lined sheet of notebook paper on which you draw a line approximately two and one half inches from the left edge of the paper. This will give you a bigger left hand column which is used for recording the main themes in the notes and adding descriptive labels and questions. The right side of the paper is used to record details about the main themes. It is helpful to use an outline format for the detail side, because it will allow you to see the relationship between the details. (see Figure 3-1)

FIGURE 3-1 The Format for the Cornell Style of Notetaking

Today's date:	Lecture topic: Taking notes from lecture

The 4 R's of note-taking

1. Be ready   1.   Be ready in mind and body

                                A. Get to class on time

                                B. Don't fall asleep in front of your professor

                  2.   Have the right materials

2. Record   1.   The Cornell style of notetaking

                                A. Write today's date before each lecture

                                B. Record the title of that day's lecture

This style of notetaking is based on finding and recording the main themes of a lecture and then supporting them with details. This means the student must isolate the main topics involved in the lecture and then show how various details support that theme. For example, in Figure 3-1, notetaking is the topic for that day's lecture which is entitled, "Taking notes from lecture." The first thing in the left hand column are the main themes that are going to be covered that day (the 4 A's of notetaking). Each of the main themes is then listed in the left column with corresponding details being recorded to the right of the drawn line. Details about each of the themes are written in outline form that show how they are related to the central idea.

One of the strongest reasons to use the Cornell Style of Notetaking is that it lends itself to recording the lecture in an organized way even when the instructor is talking fast or when the student is not sure of what is being said. Some of the biggest problems students have when taking notes is that they are not quite sure about what the main themes of the lecture are while they are actually taking the notes. The Cornell Style allows the student to go back after the lecture and add information they may have been unsure of while taking notes. The student can just write all their information on the right hand side of the line and then go back later and add the main ideas to the left side. If the student is still unsure of the main topics after reviewing his or her notes, they may be able to get this information from a classmate's notes or from the textbook.

Labeling

Using labels with the Cornell style of note taking is another helpful technique. Labeling means to add ideas to the notes that indicate that certain types of ideas are being represented, like definitions, examples or new ideas. Labels can be used as shown in **Figure 3-2** by using abbreviations on the left side of the drawn line.

FIGURE 3-2:   Labeling the Cornell Style of Notetaking

Today date:	Lecture topic: Taking notes from lecture

The 4 R's of note-taking

1. <u>Be ready</u>	1. Be ready in mind and body
Def.→	A. Means to go to every class and be alert.
Ex.→	B. Get to class on time. Don't be even a few minutes late or the professor will notice.
	C. Don't fall asleep in front of your professor
	2. Have the right materials
N.I.→	A. Use a three ring binder
	1) Replace pages that need to be edited.
	2) Place handouts or other material in the right place.
	B. Use the correct pen
2. <u>Record</u>	1. The Cornell style of notetaking
	A. Write today date before each lecture
	B. Record the title of that days lecture
	2. Use the label that gives the most information

These labels clarify the information, by showing what kind of details are being placed on the right side; the details shown in **fig 3-2** are a definition of a particular idea (**Def.**—*), an example or explanation that is being used (**Ex.**—*) and that a new idea is being introduced (**N.I**—*). There are many other labels you can use, some of them you may want to make up yourself. But make sure you understand what they mean and that you use them consistently in your notetaking.

Another way to indicate the type of material being presented is to use different colored highlighters. For example, you might use a yellow highlighter to show new vocabulary or use a blue highlighter to indicate an example is being given. The highlighting is usually done during the editing process after the lecture. There probably will not be sufficient time while the instructor is lecturing.

When the Instructor Talks Too Fast

When you first get to college, you might feel like all your professors are lecturing at 'light speed'and there is no way to get the notes down in an organized or coherent manner. Recording lecture notes seems an impossibility and you are in the wrong place at the wrong time. It may feel that way for a while, but it does become easier especially with practice and by using some of the following techniques:

- While using the Cornell Style of notetaking, make sure that you leave a lot of open space on the paper so that you can fill in later.
- Use abbreviations to speed up your writing. There are any number of abbreviations that can help. Some are generic and some are particular to a course. For example you would not want to write out the word psychology, psychologist or psychological in a Psychology class it would be much faster to use the abbreviation psy and know which psy you meant by the context of the abbreviation (**see Figure 3-3**).
  Also keep a running record of your abbreviations in the back of each section of your notebook. This will allow you to refer to them when you need to and add new abbreviations as you go. Once you have practiced this style for a while, it can become very easy and natural for you.
- Write down only the important material.

FIGURE 3-3 Abbreviations to use when the professor talks fast.

Generic	abbreviations	Abbreviations for specific courses- ex. Psychology	
with	w /	psychology	psy
without	w/o	psychologist	psy
and so on	....	psychological	psy
and	&	therapy	thrp
equal	=	behavior	bhvr
number	#	client	clnt
percent	%	stage	stg
the	T	symptom	symp
at	@	physical	phys
money	$	reward	rwd
because	→	punishment	pun
important	impt	dream	drm
question	?	cognitive	cogn
example	ex.	Emotion	emo

How Do You Know What is Important?

Most professors try to be very clear when indicating what they think is important. You can tell what is important in a lecture when the instructor actually tells you it is important. There have been any number of times when we have told a class, "This is important to remember" or, "This is the kind of information you will find on the next test," and then go back to check a student's notes and find that it had been missed. If a professor tells you something is important, or indicates that you should know it, be sure to get it in your notes.

A second way to decide if material is important is if the professor writes the information on the blackboard or on a PowerPoint©. They usually take this material directly from their notes, so there is a good chance they will use it on the next exam. Remember, if the professor writes it, you write it.
A third way you can tell if the material is important is by the emphasis given by the instructor. If they spend a lot of time on a subject or if they appear more excited or interested in a particular topic, this is the type of clue that tells you that this is potential test material.

A fourth way you can tell if something is important is if it is also discussed in your textbook. Some students find it beneficial to keep their textbook open as they take notes from the lecture particularly if the teacher follows the format of the textbook. If it is in your lecture and in the textbook, the third place you are likely to find it is on your next test. Be aware of what is going into your notes, then cross check them against your textbook or any other written material your instructor has indicated as important. This is a tried and true way of determining if the material is important.

RESTRUCTURE YOUR NOTES

The third **R** in notetaking is restructuring your notes. This means to fill in the blanks, clear up confusing passages or relate the lecture to other resources such as the textbook or other readings. Restructuring has three main purposes:

First, it gives you a chance to fill in missing material that has been given during a lecture.

Second, it allows you to emphasize what is important by editing out what is less important and to clarify confusing or misunderstood passages within the notes.

Third, it is the time to match up information given in the textbook with the ideas that have been presented in the lecture.

Fill in the Blank Spaces

How do you go about filling in the blanks? It is important for you to know where a blank occurs. One method that works for many students is indicating in the notes themselves that something is missing or confusing. **(Figure 3-4)** There are at least two ways to indicate to yourself that your notes are not complete or are incorrect. First, leave blank space in your notes where you think there is a problem. Leaving a lot of white space is a good idea when you're not sure about what is being said. If there are problems, you can then go back and fill in the missing information later. Second, use a big "?" to show that this area of your notes is confusing or needs additional work.

Once you have identified where the problem areas are, you can go back and check with another student's notes and find out what was said. If you have been using a tape recorder, you can also get the missing material from this source, but be careful. Don't rely on the tape recorder. It will not give you the whole picture. Just use it as a backup source of information.

The Cornell Style of notetaking is also helpful during the restructuring phase. Because each lecture is labeled by date and by title, it allows the student to know the exact spot where the material is missing.

Editing the Lecture

Editing can take two forms. You can take out material that is redundant or you can add new material that clarifies existing information. Editing out may be the more difficult process because it is always hard to know what an instructor thinks is important. However, there are some clues that you can use to prioritized information and give yourself a guide for studying.

We have already mentioned a few ways to determine what is important, so how do you know what is less important? If the instructor does not spend a lot of time or does not seem to be emphasizing the material this may be a clue that it will not be used on the next exam. Another way you may begin to prioritized information is by determining how it came up in class. Sometimes a student will ask a question which doesn't seem directly on topic, yet the professor goes ahead and gives an answer or explanation about it. This again can be a clue that this was not a subject the instructor had planned to discuss and therefore has less of a chance of being on a test. One way you can indicate this in your notes is by placing the acronym ASQ (answer to student question) on the left side of your notes.

The second part of the editing process is the clarification of confusing passages. These are easier to find, but still pose a problem for the notetaker. What good are notes that you don't understand? Sometimes a student just doesn't understand the example the professor has used to explain a particular idea or concept. Using examples or applications to demonstrate a specific point is a common technique used by instructors. Therefore, the student could solve the problem by finding an example about the idea or concept that they did understand. If the professor is following a textbook, the textbook will probably have other examples that deal with the same information. The textbook example may clear up the student's problem.

If they don't, the student needs to find another source that will help them. The best source to explain or clear up a specific area is the professor. During the next class, ask for other examples or ideas that might help you to understand the problem better. If you are going to use this technique, you must make sure you are going over your notes between every class. Sometimes, if you start asking questions that were covered a while back in the semester, the instructor may feel you are not keeping up with the work.

Another source you may use to clarify confusing notes is other classmates. The best way to do this is to form study groups. Sometimes, your professor, as a part of his or her class, will have groups form. If they do, make sure you take full advantage of them. However, most classes will not have a formal study group attached to them, therefore it may be up to you to get one together. These groups can really be helpful. Not only do they give you a way to clear up your notes, they can offer assistance when studying for exams or when you are preparing a project or paper.

At other times it may not be possible to form study groups. You still don't want to be left on your own. Ask around the class. See if another student will be willing to go over their notes with you. Of course, it's best to find a classmate who attends the class regularly and is a good student. Over- all you want to have some way to check over your lecture notes. You want to make sure that they are complete and correct.

REVIEW YOUR NOTES

The final **R** in taking notes from lecture is review. Although this may sound like a broken record, or should we say C.D., the review process should begin very early in the semester. You need to start learning your notes as soon as you get them. Part of the way to learn your notes is to follow the techniques discussed earlier in the first three R's. <u>The more that you work with your notes, the more familiar they are going to be.</u> The next step in the process is to put the facts and ideas into your long term memory. It takes time and repetition to learn new material. You will need to create study tools and you will need to be persistent in trying to learn the new material, but with effort and a strong plan, you can become the student you want to be.

It probably seems that all of your studying has no other purpose other than passing the next test and passing the next test is important. However, the knowledge that you gain from your notes is not exclusively for passing your college exam. The more information you keep, the richer your life will be. Information gives you choices and choices give you freedom.

Using Your Notes to Study for Exams

Using your notes to study for an examination is a talent you can acquire. An important part of this process is having a good tool to use when you start your studying. As we have just gone over, your lecture notes are an important part of your study routine. They need to be clear, concise and complete. However, that is not all you can do to assist you in your quest for an "A." You can augment your notes by using some other techniques that will help you learn the material:

- Do not try to memorize your notes. You will never remember all of the material for the test and you will probably forget most of the information after the test is over.
- Try to concentrate and focus your attention on the most important information. Just as we discussed in the chapter "**How To Read A College Textbook,**" remember to learn material from large concepts to small facts. All the information is not equal.
- Use highlighters to tell you what is important. As you did with the textbook, use different color highlighters to indicate certain types of material like vocabulary or examples. Use highlighters to indicate key words that help you remember important concepts. Sometimes, there will be words or phrases within your notes that have special meaning to you. They seem to unlock the idea behind the concept being cited. If you find words or phrases like this within your notes, make sure you let yourself know by highlighting.
- Try using flashcards to help you learn material for an exam. You can create an efficient flashcard by using 3" by 5" index cards as a tool. Using flashcards can be an extremely efficient way to learn new material. Here are some good reasons to use them:

   1. There are two important concepts that you will have to incorporate into your flashcards. First, you need to make them a tool that you can study from. It has to make you answer questions, and then give you quick

answers so that you know whether you know the fact or vocabulary idea immediately. Second it has to test more than one area of understanding, such as rote (simply memorizing facts), conceptual (placing facts into a context), or application (using the examples in a new context) learning.

2. You can carry them around and use them when you have a few spare moments.
3. They can provide you with more than one type of information, especially when you are learning new vocabulary.
4. You can separate the cards into logical groups of information. Then you can quiz yourself to see if you know the material. The information you know you can put away for review. The information you don't know needs additional work.

FIGURE 3-5 HOW TO CREATE A FLASHCARD

Create a flashcard to build a vocabulary and to learn new ideas. To make a flashcard file, you need to know how to make a flashcard that works. To make a flashcard, you use a 3" by 5" index card. On the front or lined side of the card, print the vocabulary word or the concept you want to learn.

_____

_____

_____

Mnemonic Devices_____

_____

_____

On the top of the back side or the blank side of the card, print the definition of the term. Be sure not to use the actual term in your definition. Leave some blank space and on the bottom of the card give an example of the term. Again be sure not to use the actual word in the example. When you construct a flashcard in this method, it makes it much easier to quiz yourself and you will be able learn both the definition and the application for that term.

Def. methods such as silly sentences or
pegging systems that are used to help
people memorize facts or ideas.

ex. A silly sentence which uses the first
letter of each word in that sentence to
stand for the first letter of a list of facts a
person is trying to memorize is called a

_____ _____.

Use a Study Guide

Try not to rewrite large sections of your lecture notes. You will be able to
fill in blank sections or clear up confusing passages, but to completely rewrite
notes is usually a waste of time. Instead, you may want to create a study guide that
will help you. Study guides can come in many forms. You can make concept maps
like the one shown in chapter five or you can make your own guide by condensing
material that is already in your notes. There are three main principles when
creating a study guide. **(FIGURE 3-6)**

1. A study guide is shorter than the original notes. You want to stick to key words
    or phrases to get the idea or concept across. Don't use full sentences.

2. The study guide should contain questions and answers that deal with the lecture
    material and other sources you will need to know about, such as the textbook,
    supplementary readings or handouts.

3. All information in the guide should be organized so that you understand it and
    can tell from which source the information came (in the lecture notes, the text,
    etc.)

FIGURE 3-6 **How to construct an efficient study guide**

What are the 4 r's of notetaking?

1. Be ready-text

2. Record notes-text

3. Restructure notes-text

4. Review your notes-text

1.   How can you be ready to take notes from lecture every class?

  a. Go to every class

  b. Pay attention in every class—Prof. will know

  c. Use a three ring binder—replace pages—notes in the right place—add textbook notes—more organized-lecture

  d. Use erasable pen—cleaner, clearer

  e. Know what's next—previous lecture—listen to prof.—check syllabus-lecture

  f. Sit front & center—make commitment—prof. notice you—see & hear prof better—lecture

EXERCISES

Exercise 3—1   Be there body and mind

Instructions: Wrote two paragraphs about what it means to be there, "Body and mind"

_____

_____

_____

_____

_____

Exercise 3—2   Materials for notetaking?

Instructions: Name three tools that will assist you when you are taking notes and describe how tools will help you.

1. _____

_____

2. _____

_____

3. _____

_____

Exercise 3—3   Labeling the Cornell Style of Notetaking

Instructions: Fill in the missing headings or details, from the following Cornell style of notetaking exercise.

Today date: ?	Lecture topic: Taking Notes from lecture

The 4 R's of note-taking

    1. <u>Be ready</u>
    Def. →

    _____

    N.I. →

    _____

    2. Record

    _____

1. Be ready in mind and body
    - A. Means to go to class every day and be alert.
    - B. Get to class on time. Don't be even a few minutes later or the professor will notice.

    - C. _____
2. Have the right materials
    - A. Use a three ring binder
        1) Replace pages that need to be edited.
        2) Place handouts or other materials in the right place.
    - B. Have the correct writing instrument

1. The Cornell style of notetaking
    - A. Write today's date before each lecture.
    - B. record the title of that days lecture.
2. Label the text with the clearest possible abbreviations.

Exercise 3—4   When the instructor talks too fast:

Instructions: Identify the blanks in the left hand column for term for terms or for abbreviations for those terms. In the right hand column, create seven terms and abbreviations for a course in College Skills.

Generic	abbreviations	Abbreviations for specific a course – College Skills
_____	w/	1.
without	_____	
and so on	……	2.
and	&	
_____	=	3.
number	#	
percent	_____	4.
the	T	
_____	@	5.
money	$	
_____	→	6.
important	_____	
question	?	7.
_____	ex.	

72

Exercise 3—5   Restructure your notes

Instructions: Give three reasons why you should restructure you notes.

1. _____

   _____

2. _____

   _____

3. _____

   _____

Exercise 3—6   Create a flashcard

Instructions: Create a flash card using the term **LABELING**. Use the strategies for both the lined side of the index card and for the blank side of the card.

_____ flash card side one _____

_____

_____

_____

_____ flash card side two _____

Def.

Ex.

Exercise 3—7 **Create a study guide for the section *"Record"* in Chapter three of this text**

Record notes from lecture

_____

_____

_____

_____

_____

_____

_____

How to Take a College Exam

| Introduction | In this chapter, you will learn how to take the different types of college exams and tests. You will read about test anxiety and how it affects your memory; you will practice some techniques to alleviate the negative |

consequences of test anxiety. You will also learn strategies that allow you to better attack the various types of college exams and tests.

| Goals | After you have completed this chapter, you will: |

- Be realistic about the impact of exams in your courses.
- Be able to minimize the negative effects of test anxiety.
- Adjust your studying habits according to the type of test you will be taking.
- Add to your critical thinking and writing skills.

| Activities/Tasks | These are the activities/tasks you will need to complete in order to reach the learning objectives. You should check off each activity/task |

as you complete it.

1. Using the syllabus from your psychology or sociology course, calculate the value of one exam in the final grade._____
2. Check your syllabus for the date of the first exam or test in the course and write up a study plan._____
3. Ask classmates to meet with you in a study group and hold at least one session (ACTION)._____
4. Anticipate any transportation or work problems that might make you late for the test. Plan accordingly._____
5. Listen carefully when the professor describes the type of exam he/she will be giving. Ask if no one else does._____
6. Read the chapter descriptions of the various types of exams/tests that may be given._____
7. Review a practice exam and determine which answers include distractors, superlatives, qualifiers, etc. as a way to increase your chances on a multiple-choice test.
8. Understand common terms used in a essay question._____
9. Write practice essays and short written responses._____
10.Bring a watch to the test (if there is no clock in the classroom) so you can pace yourself as you answer the questions. DO NOT PLAN TO USE YOUR CELL PHONE._____
11. Read and think about the critical thinking exercises._____

Learning Objectives	These are the assignments you need to show or submit to your instructor.

1. Make a list of the appropriate study tools you should use based on the type of test you are taking. Complete the chapter exercise and submit to your instructor.
2. Participate in a class discussion on how to distribute your time during an exam or test. Complete the chapter exercise and submit to your instructor.
3. Complete the chapter exercise on eliminating the incorrect answers to a multiple-choice question. Submit to your instructor.
4. During a class session, participate in a group study session.
5. Write an essay answer using the techniques presented in the textbook, using a question that would be appropriate for one of your lecture courses. Submit to your instructor.
6. In a small group session, create three flash cards using terms that might be found in an essay test question. Show to your instructor.
7. Complete the critical thinking exercises.
8. Answer or add at least one General Knowledge question.

Chapter Four:
How To Take a College Exam (or Test)

TEST ANXIETY

The dreaded day that usually occurs about four or five weeks into the first semester! The day when you sit down at a one-armed student desk and the professor says, "Please, take all papers from the top of your desk and store them in your bookbag or under your chair." The day of anxiety and truth! You're about to take your first college exam!

What does it mean to take an exam? To some students this is an extremely difficult and painful experience. It's a night before that is filled with anxiety. It's staying up late and trying to cram as much information into their heads as possible. As we have discussed in earlier chapters, cramming for an exam is the least effective method for learning new information. It is also the most stress producing. Many times students get themselves into a situation where they have put off studying for the exam until the last moment and cramming is their last resort.

Because not studying consistently brings about poor results, which ultimately causes even more anxiety, students need to learn how to budget their time and become more realistic about an exam's results. A realistic view of what the test means can help a student lessen their anxiety and allow them to use their study time more wisely.

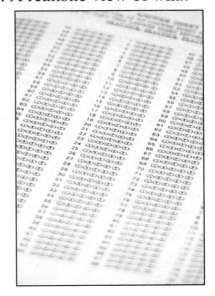

An example of unrealistic thinking follows:

"I need to pass this test."

"If I don't pass this test, I'll flunk the course"

"If I flunk the course, I won't graduate from college."

"If I don't graduate from college, I won't get a good job and then I'll end up having a miserable life."

This scenario may seem to be exaggerated, but many students put unrealistic pressure on themselves. Flunking an exam is not the end of the world. It is just one test. Most people will have many opportunities to accomplish their goals They need to stop doing things that are self-defeating and realize that trying and having a positive attitude are the best ways to accomplish their goals. Test anxiety is a real thing. As discussed in chapter one, when dealing with stress, you have to know that it can happen and try to do something about it. It is something that can delay you from getting to where you want to go. The best way to reduce test anxiety is to be prepared. You need to study as much as possible, even overstudy. You need to be confident that you know the material.

HOW TO TAKE A COLLEGE EXAM

Taking an exam in college is a skill that can be learned. In high school, studying for a test could mean nothing more than reading over a chapter once and maybe looking over some notes or going over some worksheets. Most college exams require a great deal more preparation and a much more serious approach if you are going to do well. Most professors expect their students to have a working understanding of the material that is being presented to them through the lectures and readings. Professors try to evaluate whether or not the student understands and can work with the material that has been presented to them. They do this by taking samples of the material they have lectured on, discussed in class or have assigned in the reading and then asking a series of questions about this material. Sometimes these questions will be in a short answer form such as multiple choice questions. At other times, the student will be asked to give either short written responses or full essay answers. Science or technical courses may even ask for a practical or lab exam. In each of these cases, the student needs to plan how they are going to master the material for the test. In chapters two and three, we discussed how you could develop such tools as your textbook and lecture notes so that they were the most effective for studying and remembering new information. The proof to see if the tools were effective lies in taking the examination itself. If the results are positive, you are on the right track. If the results were disappointing, you need to go back and re-examine your study tools and your study method.

HOW TO STUDY FOR AN EXAM

If you have been following your study plan you are well on your way to being prepared for the test. Remember, you don't want to wait until the last day to cram information into your head. The last week before the test should be used primarily for your final review. You should gather all your materials together:

- your marked textbook
- your complete and highlighted notes
- flashcards
- concept map
- study guide

and any other material that is relevant to the exam. Go over your material by testing yourself. See if you can predict questions that will be on the exam. You should try to put these questions in the form in which you will see them on the exam. If your professor uses primarily multiple choice questions, see if you can pick out the kind of detail that might be included in a multiple choice test, including what kinds of detail could throw you off. Also, look for information that lends itself to essay questions if the professor uses this form of questioning. You might ask, "How do I go about finding out what kinds of questions there will be on the test." The best way is to ask the professor. Most teachers don't mind or may even make it a practice to tell their classes what kind of test they give. They may even be specific about it and tell you what type and how many questions there are on the test. But the trick is to know as early in the course as possible if you plan to use the information to study.

USE STUDY GROUPS TO PREPARE FOR EXAMS

Another good way to prepare for an exam is to use study groups. As was discussed in chapter three, study groups can help you to pick out what is important in the material you are given. In addition, a study group can help each member by cutting down the amount of preparation work that needs to be done. This can be accomplished by having each person in the group responsible for, or become the expert on, a section of the information that will be covered in the exam. When the group gets together, each member of the group can act as a leader and help the rest of the group with their particular section. Also, each person in the group should construct a study tool for their area of the material and make a photocopy of it so that each member will have a series of study tools for the entire test.

THE DAY OF THE EXAM

On the day of the test, you should be sure to be on time or early for the examination. You should have had a good night's sleep, because you didn't cram. Also, you should have had something to eat. Don't eat too much, but make sure that you are comfortable. You want to get rid of as many distractions as possible. If the classroom is usually chilly, bring a sweater. If it's warm, layer your clothing so you can remove pieces if you're uncomfortable. The most important thing for you to remember, however, is to get there early enough so that you can get settled before the test is handed out. Getting in late will:

- upset your professor
- cut into the time you have to take the test
- increase your own anxiety
- disrupt the rest of your classmates

SURVEY THE TEST FIRST

Before you answer the first question, look through the entire test and see how many points are being given. For example, if the test has fifty multiple choice questions worth one point each, and two essay questions worth twenty- five a piece, you will need to know how to budget your time (bring a watch if there is no visible clock). If you have one hour to take the exam, you need to spend about thirty minutes on the essays. You don't want to be forty minutes into a sixty minute exam and just be finishing your multiple choice questions. Since each area is worth 50% of the exam, you want to spend approximately one half of your time on each section. Also, as you survey your exam, make sure that you read all of the directions. You don't want to complete the third essay only to find out that you were only supposed to do two out of the three.

Lastly, when you are surveying a test to see if the questions are in order or if they overlap, you might want to check to see if the test follows the order of the chapters in the textbook. Sometimes instructors will use tests that are constructed by the textbook's author/company and they will come in a specific order: chapter one questions, chapter two questions, chapter three questions, etc., especially when the tests are multiple choice only. It can sometimes help you avoid mixing up information if you know what chapter they are taken from.

Also, particularly in a multiple choice test which also has essays, you should look for an overlap in information. Sometimes, a question asked in the multiple choice section will help you to remember a detail that will enhance an essay. The helpful information in the multiple choice questions doesn't even have to be the correct answer to a particular question. It could be a distracter.

When surveying, you should spend approximately four minutes for a sixty minute test. For longer test periods, you can expand that time proportionately. Also, if you sit up front, you may save a couple of minutes because they usually give tests out from front to back. And, you'll get to read the test a couple of minutes early.

TAKING THE EXAM—MULTIPLE CHOICE

A multiple choice question is one that gives the correct answer to the student along with three or four distracting answers which are incorrect. The student is asked to pick out the correct answer among the three or four choices. In this example, the distracters are relatively easy to pick out.

FIGURE 4-1 **MULTIPLE CHOICE QUESTION**

A large cat of prey is called a _____.
  a. Cow
  b. Lion
  c. Kitten
  d. Jackal

Often you will find in multiple choice tests that the distracters are chosen so that one will be very far from the correct answer like the choice, **a. cow** in Figure 4-1; a second distracter is closer to being correct like the choice, **c. kitten** and one distracter may be very close to the correct answer and is the most difficult for the student to make a decision about like, **d. jackal**. Later on in this section, there will be some techniques that will help you to make decisions about whether an answer is a distracter or not.

Multiple choice exams are very popular with many college instructors, especially in the Freshman and Sophomore years. They are popular because they are easy to grade and lend themselves to electronic grading machines. The instructor may also ask questions that test your understanding of the material in several different ways. Sometimes, students get confused when reading a multiple choice question because they are not used to seeing questions worded in a new way. The most common area of confusion comes when a teacher asks application type questions. Most students don't get much experience in high school answering questions like this. An application question is one which cites an example and asks the student to match that example with an idea, concept or theory. (**see FIGURE 4-2**) The greatest problem comes for many students with the usage of language. In FIGURE 4-2, the question begins by posing a scenario. "John is a four year old boy. . . ." A student may get confused because the question is not asked in the usual style, i.e., What type of thought would Piaget call the inability to distinguish class inclusion? This question is looking for a connection between an idea and an action or example.

FIGURE 4-2 MULTIPLE CHOICE APPLICATION QUESTION

John is a four year old boy who is given twenty red wooden beads and five yellow wooden beads. When asked whether there are more red beads or wooden beads, John responds, "There are more red beads." John's reasoning is an example of what Piaget calls _____ thought.
   a. formal operational
   b. preoperational
   c. egocentric
   d. intuitive

Another way a student can get confused is by not reading all the possible choices. Many times students will read a question and read a. then b. and come to what he or she considers the correct answer. In FIGURE 4.3, a student may read this, see the answer "California", and say to themselves, "That's correct", and circle that as the right answer. If he or she had read all of the possible answers, they would have come to D. Hollywood and realized that this would be a better answer because it is more specific. An important technique to remember when taking a multiple choice test is to read all the possible answers so you can choose wisely. There may be more than one correct answer, so it is up to the student to find the best one.

FIGURE 4-3 **READ ALL ANSWERS BEFORE CHOOSING**

Where are most of the major movie studios located?
a. New York
b. California
c. Chicago
d. Hollywood

INCREASE YOUR CHANCES ON A MULTIPLE CHOICE TEST

Another technique you can use to help you get a better grade on a multiple choice test is to reduce the number of answers you have to choose from. As was mentioned earlier in the section, multiple choice questions are usually constructed with three distracters, with each of the distracters coming closer to the correct answer. If you could eliminate a couple of these answers, you greatly improve your chances of getting the question correct. For example, looking back at (**FIGURE 4.3**), if you did not know the correct answer but had a general idea about where movies were made, you could probably eliminate Chicago and New York as answers. This will leave you just two choices, California or Hollywood. Even if you don't know the answer, you have doubled your chance of getting it correct, and over the course of a test, this could mean a full grade improvement.

The following are a series of additional techniques you can use to eliminate distracters or identify the two answers that are the closest to being the correct answer.
- "**All of the above**"—When one of the answers to a multiple choice question is "All of the above" there is a high percentage chance that it will be the correct answer, particularly if the test comes from a textbook prepared test bank. Even if you can identity one of the other three answers as incorrect, then you have eliminated two distracters ("All of the above" and the other answer you identified as being incorrect).
- **When two of the terms look or sound similar, they may be the two best answers**. For example, Bismarck is the capital of A. North Dakota B. South Dakota C. Kansas D. Florida" the question will probably be trying to have you discriminate between North and South Dakota.
- **When superlatives are used, the answer is probably incorrect**. A superlative is a word like 'never' or 'all' which leaves no room for any exception. Therefore, most teachers do not include this type of answer as a

correct answer. However, they may use them as distracters which will allow you to exclude them. (**see FIGURE 4-4**)

- **Look for qualifiers, they may be the correct answer**. Qualifiers are words and phrases like most of the time, generally, usually, and in many cases. This is done because they know that most questions have exceptions therefore this method eliminates that error. (**see FIGURE 4-5**)

- **Sometimes instructors will use vocabulary you have not seen before as distracters.** If you have not seen the word before, do not choose it as an answer. Sometimes, however the unfamiliar word may be the correct answer and this means you overlooked it in your studying.

- **Use common sense**. If you're not sure of the correct answer, see if you can find the wrong one. If you can find at least one wrong answer, it still improves your chances.

- **Use mnemonic devices for multiple choice questions in a series**. Some questions lend themselves to being asked in a series, such as stages in a psychological theory or the animal orders in Biology. Use a mnemonic device like an acronym to help you remember. (Mnemonic devices will be discussed in Chapter five)

- **None of the above** is not as common an answer as many of the others described, however, occasionally, a professor may use it. The best way to handle questions when 'none of the above' is one of your choices is to first look for an answer that could be correct. If you find at least one answer that could be correct, then you can eliminate the answer 'none of the above.'

- **Above all, make sure you answer all questions**. With an answer, you still have a chance of getting the question right.

FIGURE 4-4 SUPERLATIVES MAY INDICATE A WRONG ANSWER

all	none	only
always	no one	absolutely not
never	nobody	everyone
perfect	invariably	everybody
best	absolutely	without exception
worst	certainly	under no circumstance

FIGURE 4-5 QUALIFIERS MAY INDICATE AN ANSWER IS CORRECT

some	frequently	probably
sometimes	most	sometimes
usually	a few	a majority of times
may	often	unlikely
may be	much	at times

MACHINE GRADED TESTS

Machine graded multiple choice tests are common at community colleges. Machine grading uses special answer sheets to grade your paper. (**see FIGURE 4-6**) These sheets are usually numbered one through fifty or one through one hundred and have five response circles for each answer (a, b, c, d, e). You pick an answer to each question and pencil in that lettered circle that indicates your answer. For most tests like this, you need a number 2 pencil. Be sure to be precise because if the machine detects more than one answer in a row, it will mark it as incorrect. Even if you erased, but not thoroughly, the machine might pick this up as an error. So bring a good eraser with your number two pencil.

Make sure that you're also answering the questions in order or have indicated on your answer sheet that you need to fill in a question that you skipped. Sometimes students will get into trouble by skipping over a question that they did not know and forget to adjust the sequence on the answer sheet. This can mean disaster. If you get out of order early in the test your answers will be out of sequence. The machine will just mark all these questions wrong. So be precise and pay attention to the order. You could save yourself a lot of trouble.

Most professors will announce the correct answers when they give back the test. Bring an extra answer sheet so that you can record the correct answers and ask it you can see which answers you got wrong. If you can see where you are making your mistakes, it will help you on tests in the future. Be in class the day the test is returned to you and learn what the right answers are. It you have had any of the problems just mentioned, this may be the time for your last appeal.

FIGURE 4-6 MACHINE GRADED TEST

Instructions: Using a #2 pencil, fill in the appropriate circle with the correct answer from your test sheet.

1. a O   b O   c O   d O   e O
2. a O   b O   c O   d O   e O
3. a O   b O   c O   d O   e O
4. a Q   b O   c O   d O   e O
5. a O   b O   c O   d O   e O

TRUE OR FALSE TEST

Usually, true or false questions are only a part of an objective test. These questions are not necessarily the easiest but they do provide you with the best chance of getting the answer correct when you are not sure of the right answer. You have a fifty percent chance of getting the question correct, so you need to answer all of these questions. There are a few techniques you can use to help you to do well on the true or false questions.

- **Read the statement thoroughly**. The correct answer may hinge on a single word.
- **Begin to read the statement with the idea that the answer is true**, then look for the words or phrases that would make them false. If you can't find anything, mark it true.
- **Look to see if the statement is negative or a double negative**. Sometimes true or false questions will ask questions using two negatives either with two words being negative such as: (Example: He is not depressed) or with one word being negative and a prefix which is negative: (Example: the girl is not unhappy.) In both cases, the question is asking for a positive answer.
- **As in multiple choice questions, look for qualifiers and superlatives**. Qualifiers tend to make statements true while superlatives tend to make questions false.

MATCHING TESTS

Matching tests are not used to a large extent on college exams, however, you may run into one or two such questions on a test and they may count for a significant number of points. Be careful and don't treat these questions lightly.

A matching test asks a student to match items from one column to items in another column. (see **FIGURE 4-7**) FIGURE 4-7 shows how statements or words in the first column relate or are answered by words or phrases in the second column. Be sure to look over all items in both columns before you begin. The best thing to do when dealing with this type of question is to connect the easier pairs first so that when you are left with the harder pairs, you have fewer choices to deal with. (FIGURE 4-7) As you match questions from the left column, you eliminate items in the right column. You may not ever know the correct match to the final pair of words or phrases, but you will be left with only one response. Therefore, the answer is given to you. Sometimes it helps to match the column which has more words in it to the column that has fewer words. (FIGURE 4-7) Also, when doing matching questions try to be logical and use common sense. If a question in the left column is asking for a person's name, then you can eliminate all responses but names. If the question in one column indicates some type of action in response, in the other column look for verbs or action phrases. Again, like any other objective question, make sure you answer all items in the question. It never hurts to give it a chance.

FIGURE 4-7 MATCHING QUESTIONS

Instructions: Match the sport with the person that is associated with that sport.

1. football	Mario Lemeux
2. track and field	Joe Paterno
3. baseball	Greg Louganis
4. diving	Monica Seles
5. tennis	John Lasorta
6. golf	Bruce Jenner
7. hockey	Tiger Woods

SHORT WRITTEN RESPONSE QUESTIONS

This type of question can take two forms. The first is called a '**fill-in- the-blank**' question. In this type of question, the student is asked to provide a missing word or words to complete a short paragraph. (**see FIGURE 4-8**). Unlike the test questions we discussed before, this type of test question does not provide the test taker with the correct answer. There is no guessing. If you don't know the answer, you're in big trouble. The student must know the correct response. The good thing about fill-in-the-blank questions is that they are always in a context that can give you clues about the answer. The following are a few techniques to look for when answering a fill-in-the-blank question.

- Does it call for more than a one word response? Many times there will be more than one blank or the directions will specify that more than one word is needed.

- Look to see if names, dates, theories or concepts are being asked for and then respond appropriately.

- See if the blank is proceeded by the letter "A" or "An." If it is preceded by "An," then you know the answer must begin with a vowel (A, E, I, 0, U). If the blank is preceded by the letter "A," then you know that your response must start with a consonant, which is any letter that is not a vowel.

- If you're not sure that your answer makes sense or you know that it is wrong, don't answer at all. Leave the question blank. This is not like the objective tests that we discussed before. If your answer to the question makes no sense, then the professor knows you are bluffing and might discount answers that are close but not exactly correct.

FIGURE 4-8 FILL-IN-THE-BLANK QUESTIONS

Instructions: Fill-in-the-blank or blanks in the following questions.

1. The final stage of Piaget's theory of cognitive development is called
   _____ _____.

2. The capital of North Dakota is _____.

The second type of short answer question is one where the student has to respond by writing a short paragraph to answer a question. This is unlike an essay because it is usually looking for a single idea or concept. The best way to approach this type of question is to begin your answer with a clearly written thesis statement or topic sentence. This will demonstrate that you understand the question and are answering it directly. Many times, these types of questions will be looking for three types of responses. First, it may be asking for a definition of an idea, theory or concept. In this type of question, you need to provide the fundamental or most important aspects of that idea, theory or concept. You don't want to get bogged down with too many small details.

The second type of response that is being called for in this type of short, written, response question is an application. Instead of just defining a particular idea, theory or concept, the student is asked to give an example of how these things work (**see FIGURE 4.9**). The third type of response that many of these types of questions ask for are lists or sequences of events. Again, a clear topic sentence should be used and then the sequence should be labeled showing how each part is separate and distinct. You can do this by labeling 1, 2, 3, 4 or A, B, C, D, but you need to show that your list or sequence is complete and distinct. Also, look to see if the question asks for a specific order like most important to least important, one date to the next or what happens first to what happens last.

FIGURE 4-9 **Short written responses**

Instructions: Briefly state how Piaget's theory of cognitive development defines assimilation and accommodation.

1. Assimilation occurs when someone incorporates new information into already existing experiences. Assimilation is the way humans build their store of knowledge. Assimilation lasts your whole life time.
2. Accommodation occurs when someone adapts new information into existing experience. Accommodation allows the individual to adjust to new things and ideas in their environment. Accommodation also lasts through a whole life time.

ESSAY EXAMS

Essay exams will be a large part of your test taking experience, especially after the freshman year. You will see essays more and more as you go on to your sophomore, junior and senior years, so it is good to get as much practice as possible while you are a freshman.

There are two major types of essay exams. The first is the kind you take in class with no outside resources and a time limit. The second type is the take-home exam. Usually, you will be given several days to complete this exam and will have access to all the books, notes and other resources you need.

THE IN-CLASS ESSAY EXAM

For the 'in-class' exam, there are a number of things you need to do to be successful.

1. You need to read the directions thoroughly and decide how much time you can spend on each essay.

2. If there is a multiple choice or other objective portion of the exam, check back to see if there is vocabulary you can use in your essay.

3. Look for specific terms that will tell you what type of essay you're supposed to write. There are some common terms used in the directions of most essay tests. **(see FIGURE 4-10)**

4. Answer the question you are most confident about first. This will help you get used to writing. It will also help your confidence. However, remember to budget your time according to the point values given. Sometimes you can get carried away with an essay you're confident about, so you spend most of your time on it and don't give yourself sufficient time for the essays that are going to give you more trouble.

5. When you start writing, be clear. Start with a topic sentence and follow up with supporting data that is directly related to the topic sentence. Don't be flowery or try to fool your instructor. They will have a pretty good idea if you understand the topic. Make a short outline on scrap paper or in the margin. This will give you some structure and will let you have a starting point and an ending point.

6. If you do get caught short of time, at least put down what you wanted to write about in outline form. This will tell your instructor that you have some understanding of the topic. It might also get you some partial credit. Write neatly and make your letters large enough for the instructor to read. Use an erasable ball-point pen so that you are not scratching out mistakes. Don't crowd your words. Leave sufficient space between them so it is easier to read.

7. Be organized—the outline will help you. The first paragraph should be introductory. It should state the emphasis of the question and delineate the parts within the question. The interior paragraphs should be supporting paragraphs. They should begin with a topic sentence and should be in some logical order. For example, if you were comparing or contrasting a particular idea you might use the first two or three interior paragraphs to contrast. Finally, the last paragraph should be used for a conclusion. The conclusion should sum up or even restate the original question.

FIGURE 4-10 COMMON TERMS USED IN THE DIRECTIONS OF ESSAY EXAMS

Discuss: Write as much as you know about the topic. Try to mention all the main points concerning the topic. Add as much detail as possible.
> Example: Discuss Freud's theory of personality development as it pertains to defense mechanisms.

Compare: Discuss similarities as well as differences between two or more topics.
> Example: Compare the effects of birth defects caused by genetics and by teratogens.

Contrast: Discuss the differences between topics.
> Example: Contrast the use of oil-based paint with the use of water-based paint when painting a still life.

Enumerate: Number or list all pertinent items of a topic.
> Example: Enumerate the causes for the Civil War.

Define: Discuss the meaning of the topic or term.
> Example: Define the term socialization.

Trace: Discuss in chronological order or order of development a topic or event.
> Example: Trace the beginnings of the women's movement from its start to today.

Explain: State reasons why something happened.
> Example: Explain why Truman thought he should drop the atomic bomb on Japan.

Outline: Make a numbered outline of a topic.
> Example: Outline the stages of Kolberg's theory of moral development.

Illustrate: Discuss a point or event using examples.
> Example: Illustrate the use of mnemonic in memory development.

THE TAKE-HOME EXAM

The second type of essay exam is a take-home exam. Generally, the instructor is looking for a much more comprehensive piece of work with this type of test. He or she will be expecting a polished and detailed essay. Again, make sure of your directions. Check to see if there are multiple parts to the essay. Also, make sure that you word process this essay. Be careful to check your grammar and your spelling. The take-home essay exam should be treated just like a major paper.

THE OPEN BOOK EXAM

When a class is asked if they would like an open book exam they invariably exclaim, "Yes!" Bad choice! Although, this may seem an easier choice, most of the time the tests are so much more difficult that you are better off facing the unknown. Also, for most of these tests you will not have sufficient time to look up all the answers. However, if you do get caught having to take an open book exam, be sure that you have put in as much study time as you would have in a regular closed book test. Also you may want to set up an indexing system for your notes and for your textbook. This can be done by using clearly labeled tabs and placing them in important areas of your notes and text. This will allow you to access information quickly if you are not sure of an answer.

THE LAB EXAM

The final type of examination we are going to discuss is the practical laboratory exam. Usually, you will get these types of exams in the sciences such as Biology, Chemistry or Physics or in courses like Allied Health or computer-related subjects.

The lab exam asks the student to describe, locate, define or demonstrate using the practical materials or subjects of the discipline. For example, in a Biology lab exam, the student may be asked to locate a chamber of the heart of a specimen they have been dissecting, using that specimen or a similar one. Another example may be in a physics lab. The student may be asked to demonstrate how the fulcrum of a lever impacts on the amount of force needed to lift a certain weight. The best way to prepare for a lab exam is to have worked in the lab as much as possible.

When taking a lab exam, be sure you understand what is being tested and how the questions are going to be asked. If there are techniques that you will be asked to demonstrate or explain, be sure that you practice them before the exam. If you're not sure, ask your professor or a student who has taken the lab before.

EXERCISES CHAPTER FOUR

Exercise 4-1   How to study for an exam

Instructions: Name five study tools you should gather together before you start studying for an exam.

1. _____

2. _____

3. _____

4. _____

5. _____

Exercise 4-2   How to distribute your time during an exam

Instructions: Indicate in the answer area, how many minutes you would spend on each area of the exam.

1. Duration of the exam 60 minutes

Type of question	number of questions	points/question
Matching	10	10
multiple choice	30	60
essay	2	30

Answers

surveying: _____

matching:_____

multiple choice:_____

essay:_____

2. Duration of the exam 90 minutes

Type of question	number of questions	points/question
multiple choice	20	30
short answer	10	20
essay	2	50

Answers

surveying:_____

multiple choice:_____

short answer:_____

essay:_____

Exercise 4-3 deciding which answers are correct/incorrect on a multiple choice exam

Instructions: Use the strategies described in the multiple choice section of this chapter to help you narrow down possible correct answers. Write the strategy or strategies you would use in the space provided after each question. Then make a guess and circle the answer you think is correct.

1. Which city is located in the state of New York?
   a. Buffalo
   b. Albany
   c. Syracuse
   d. all of the above

2. What newspaper uses the slogan "All the news that is fit to print"
   a. The New York Daily News
   b. The Philadelphia Inquirer
   c. The New York Times
   d. The Washington Post

3. Name the sport that uses a birdie.
   a. Tennis
   b. Badminton
   c. Baseball
   d. all of the above

4. Which side of the brain is most associated with language?
   a. the brain stem
   b. the right hemisphere
   c. the hippocampus
   d. the left hemisphere

5. What is the most prevalent type of family structure in America?
   a. single parent families
   b. extended families
   c. nuclear families
   d. detriangulation families

6. The great majority of police officers are men, this is probably because:
   a. Women don't want to be police officers.
   b. Men make the best police officers.
   c. Women are not expected to be police officers.
   d. Many women find other occupations more attractive.

7. What painter in the Impressionist school is known for his studies of water lilies?
   a. Monet
   b. Picasso
   c. Manet
   d. Rembrandt

8. The tortured painter Van Gogh, who cut off his ear and sent it to his lover, was know for:
   a. Always using the color yellow
   b. Never finishing a painting
   c. Usually using bold colors and broad brush strokes
   d. Using unusual paint brushes

9. The most common dog in America is:
   a. the poodle
   b. the collie
   c. the bulldog
   d. some weirdly named dog

Exercise 4-4   How to attack a matching question on an exam

Instructions: Use the strategies and clues discussed in the matching section of this chapter to complete the following questions.

1.	What psychologist is most associated with radical behaviorism?	Piaget
2.	A defense mechanism	assimilation
3.	What psychologist described the term "the proximal zone"?	Behaviorism
4.	What cognitive psychologist developed a stage theory of cognitive development?	Vygotsky
5.	A cognitive adaptation term	reinforcement
6.	A theory that stated that behavior was the most	displacement
7.	The first psychosexual stage in Freud theory	Skinner
8.	The term used by behaviorist to describe what actions prompt behavior from another	oral

Exercise 4-5   Short written responses

Instructions: Write a one paragraph answer to the following questions. Remember to use a strong topic sentence.

1. Why are machine-graded tests attractive to some teachers?

2. How does a study group help you learn new material?

3. Why is it important to get to the test early?

4. What are three things you do when you survey a test you are going to take?

5. Give two reasons why a student could become confused on a multiple choice exam.

Exercise 4-6   Terms used in essays

Instructions: Briefly describe what the following terms mean when they are written in an essay question.

1. Discuss _____

_____

2. Compare _____

_____

3. Trace _____

_____

4. Illustrate _____

_____

5. Contrast _____

_____

98

Improving Your Memory

| Introduction | In this chapter you will learn how memory works and ways to improve your memory. This will make your study time more efficient and effective. Specific techniques will be described that help you organize and store information. |

| Goals | After you have completed the work in this chapter you will: |

- Feel more confident in your ability to learn and memorize information.
- Approach note taking and study with techniques that help you see the relationships between factual information.
- Learn and study more efficiently and effectively.

| Activities/Tasks | This section describes the steps you need to take to complete the activities/tasks in the chapter. You should check off each activity/task as you complete it. |

1. Read and take notes on the section of the chapter on how memory works._____
2. Work with a classmate to develop an "association" exercise that increases short-term memory._____
3. Organize the types of memory found in long term memory into a schematic or flow chart._____
4. Read the section concerning problems with memory and techniques to improve memory._____
5. Using a section of your psychology or sociology book, develop visual images to help you remember the important terms._____
6. Create a concept map for a section of your psychology or sociology book._____
7. Go to an office on campus (library, student services, President's Office, Human Resources, etc.) and ask for a copy of the organizational flow chart (ACTION)_____
8. Working with a classmate or friend, develop mnemonic devices for two concepts you are required to learn._____
9. Develop an acronym and a sentence for information you are currently learning in psychology or sociology class._____
10. Find or develop a rhyme that incorporates material you are learning._____
11. Find or develop a pegging system for a series of facts you are learning._____
12. Answer or add at least one general knowledge question._____
13. Read, think about and respond to the critical thinking exerices._____

Learning Objectives	These are the assignments you need to complete and show or hand in to your instructor.

1. Participate in a class activity to develop an association exercise, visual images, mnemonic devices, acronyms, rhyme, pegging system and sentence for material you are now learning.
2. Turn in an organizational chart of an office or department on campus.
3. Submit the independent work on memory improvement techniques along with the activities completed in class (#1 above).
4. Complete and submit the chapter exercises which include stages of memory, concept map, planner acronyms, and sentence. (Use the acronym and sentence from #1 above).
5. Write and submit an essay on the techniques of persuasion (Critical Thinking).
6. Answer or add at least one general education question.

Chapter Five: How To Improve Your Memory

INTRODUCTION

Do you become frustrated when you study for an exam the night before and then "forget" all the material by exam time? Are you surprised at the information (phone numbers, addresses, concert dates) that you do remember? This chapter looks at these questions and gives you some hints on how to improve your memory.

It is important to know how your memory works if you are going to try to improve it. Some people believe memory is genetic and think that their memory is unchangeable and they must go with the hand they were dealt. Contrary to this belief, although genetics do play a role in memory, it is not the only factor. You can increase your ability to store and retrieve information. Your memory can be improved; however, most people have either not been shown how to use their memory or have not taken the opportunity to improve it.

There are four major keys to improving your memory:

1. You must want to improve your memory. You must make a concerted effort to increase your storage and retrieval systems.
2. You must know how the memory works so that you can implement ways to improve it.
3. You must practice techniques such as active listening, increased attention and using mnemonic devices that are designed to increase memory.
4. You must be patient with yourself and be positive about increasing your memory. It takes time to improve your memory. Not all people improve at the same rate. You can not become discouraged or lose motivation if you don't double your memory capacity overnight. The idea to hang on to is that it you work hard and are patient, you will have a better memory.

HOW MEMORY WORKS

This section is designed to explore how the memory works. The memory can be looked at as if it were an information processing system. Each of these components is important for the storage of information. This system is made up of three basic components:

1. sensory memory
2. short-term memory
3. long-term memory

FIGURE 5-1 **HOW THE BRAIN PROCESSES INFORMATION**

SIGHT   →   **SENSORY MEMORY**
HEARING →   **SHORT-TERM MEMORY**
                        LONG TERM MEMORY   →   **SEMANTIC**
                                                                   →   **PROCEDURAL**
                                                                   →   **EPISODIC**

SENSORY MEMORY

Sensory memory is the beginning of memory. All of our sensory organs pick up things from the environment and start processing them towards the brain. The two main learning senses that humans use are the sense of sight and the sense of sound. In other words, humans tend to learn and remember by seeing or hearing things. The sensory memory is not retained for long, perhaps only one half to three or four seconds. The signal is then either transferred into short-term memory or is ignored. This makes a lot of sense. If we were to process each little bit of stimulation from the environment we would go crazy. If you heard the sound of a door shutting or saw the flicker of light as a window shade blew open and had to keep this in your mind for long periods of time, you would not be able to concentrate on anyone particular thing. So the key to moving information from sensory memory to short term memory is to pay attention to something you've heard or seen. (**see FIGURE 5.1**)

As you will see, paying attention and trying to remember plays a very big role in how well you will be able to remember something in the future.

SHORT-TERM/WORKING MEMORY

Once you have attended to a piece of information, it goes into short- term memory. Short-term memory is also short in duration, approximately twenty to thirty seconds in length. Short-term memory is sometimes compared to a leaky bucket because as more information comes in, other information leaks out. For example, think of when you go into a phone booth and look up a number from the phone book. The genius who designed the phone booth attached the phone book so that you couldn't keep the book open and also dial the number. So what do you do? You find the number and then begin repeating it to yourself until you punch in the correct numbers. The instant the last number is punched in, for most people, is the last recollection of that number. You don't need it any more and it is gone from short-term memory. So, the trick to keeping new information or putting it into long-term memory is rehearsing the material over and over or writing it down so that you can practice it over a period of time.

Another interesting characteristic of short-term memory is its capacity. For most people, short-term memory holds about five to nine pieces or bits of information at a time with an average of seven bits. For example, if you were given a set of numbers or letters to remember, most people would recall about seven of these before they began forgetting. However, the brain works in an interesting manner. If you combine bits of information so that the bits form an association, the short-term memory will remember about seven chunks of information. In FIGURE 5.2, when the letters are combined into words, (bits of information that are associated), they are just as easily memorized.

FIGURE 5-2 ASSOCIATION INCREASES THE CAPACITY OF SHORT-TERM MEMORY

If someone were trying to memorize thirty bits of information in order, like the letters below, they would probably have a very difficult time without a lot of practice.

1. **hetgoddepmujaecnefevifteefhgIh**
However, if you organized the bits of information into groups or words, memorizing the material is much easier, as shown below:

2. **The dog jumped a fence five feet high**.
The sentence above is made up from the letters contained in group #1.

LONG-TERM MEMORY

Long-term memory is the inception of cognition; it is the beginning of understanding. Long-term memory allows humans to make choices about their future. They can reflect on their past and project into their future to see a course of action for themselves.

There are three basic types of long-term memory:

1. Semantic Memory—which is the memory of information and skills like the ones you would learn in school or on a job.
2. Procedural Memory—which is more connected to physical learning such as how to ride a bike or use a pen.
3. Episodic Memory—which deals with specific events in a person's life. These are usually related to experience which have an emotional impact on the individual.

We are mostly concerned with semantic memory and the retrieval of information from the long-term memory. The most important keys to getting retrievable information into long-term semantic memory are based around three interrelated factors:

1. *The organization of the information being learned.*

The organization of information is important to remembering because the brain is better able to remember material that is linked together. Just as in short-term memory, the brain seems to be able to process a group of related facts or information as easily as it processes a single item. When we are trying to put material into long-term memory, it helps to organize it into connecting packages. This is called clustering. There are a number of techniques that will be discussed later in the chapter that can help you organize information.

2. *The association of new information with material previously learned.*

As we discussed earlier, association also helps the brain to remember and retrieve information. Again, when a person tries to remember something, it is easier to recall it when it is associated with things that are already learned, particularly when it is connected to an area or subject that is familiar to the learner. The more you know, the easier it is to add new information. For example, in the sport of basketball, when a new rule is introduced to the game, like the three point basket or the shortening of time to shoot, most players don't have a difficult time remembering these new rules, because it is just a small part of a much larger group of information.

3. *The visualization of the new material being learned.*

Visualization is a third factor that helps the brain to remember. The brain seems to remember things in pictures as opposed to in symbols. For example, if you read the word 'tree' in a book, the brain does not store the symbol "TREE," it stores a particular picture of a tree. There is evidence that indicates that if you can create pictures of the information, you will have a much better chance of retrieving it later.

PROBLEMS WITH MEMORY AND TECHNIQUES TO IMPROVE IT

Why do students have memory problems? There are many things that can interfere with the memory. Forgetting is a natural process. Researchers have shown that most people forget 70% of what they have experienced within forty-eight hours. People need to forget because they are processing information all the time. Our brains use forgetting as a clearing house. It gets rid of all of the information that is not essential. Unfortunately, if we don't practice remembering techniques, the brain will also get rid of information we would like to keep. The following are ways forgetting occurs:

- The most common way people forget is that they don't try to remember. For example, when you go to a party and people are being introduced to you, if you don't try to remember their names, as you meet them again, most likely you won't be able to remember those names.
- A second cause of forgetting is the passing of time. Many things we have learned seem to decay in time if they are not used. If you learned Algebra in high school and then did not use it very much afterward, you would probably forget a good portion of what you learned.
- A third way people forget is from interference. There are two major types of interference, proactive interference and retroactive interference. Proactive

interference means that as more and more information comes in, there is a tendency to push out old information. For example, if you were trying to learn a list of words, as more and more words were added to the list, you would have a tendency to start to forget words already learned. Retroactive interference means old information can interfere with new material being learned. An example of this might be if you were beginning to drive a car in England, where they drive on the left side of the road, the fact that you are used to driving a car in America on the right side of the road might interfere with you consistently remembering on which side you are to drive in England.

TECHNIQUES TO IMPROVE YOUR MEMORY

As was discussed earlier in this chapter, many of the techniques that help memory are based on the interrelated factors of organization, association and visualization. Let's take, for example, how we could solve some of the problems that were presented in the section of this chapter entitled "PROBLEMS WITH MEMORY." One of the first problems we encounter when we begin to forget was illustrated by the example of how we forget names at a party. The best technique for solving this problem is to go to the party with the idea that you are going to try to remember people's names. Make an effort to listen to their name and then to repeat it. In addition, you could try to associate some physical or personal characteristic to the name of that person. For instance, if the person's name was Linda and she is thin or has a narrow face or nose, you might want to visualize that characteristic and associate it with the name "**Lean-da**."

Another problem we encounter with forgetting is that the things we learn seemed to fade away or decay as time passed. The way we can counter this problem is to first try to practice things that we believe are valuable even when we do not have a current use for them. Another way to respond to this problem is to keep a journal about what keys helped you learn the material in the first place. This will help you relearn it if the time comes when you need it again. Also, it is easier for most people to relearn information. They can usually learn it much faster. Writing information down can especially help the college student. It will be very difficult to remember what was said in a lecture about Freud if the student doesn't take complete notes as the professor lectures. Writing allows the student to get this information and then organize it so that they can make sense of the information later. Writing it down also allows the student to go back and review the material as many times as necessary. Other methods that can help you learn new material are found in the following section.

CONCEPT MAPS

The concept map allows the student to organize, associate and visualize new information all at the same time. The strength of the concept map is that it not only allows you to make judgments about what is important, but it allows you to see the relationships between ideas. This is an extremely important part of remembering. It is very difficult for many students to see how ideas connect but that connection is the most important point. It is so much more difficult to remember things that have no relevance. So, to give information a sense of order or importance, it is a good idea to use a concept map. **See FIGURE 5-3**. Not only does it show how information flows in terms of importance, it also shows how each part relates to all the other parts of the concept.

FIGURE 5-3 **A CONCEPT MAP**

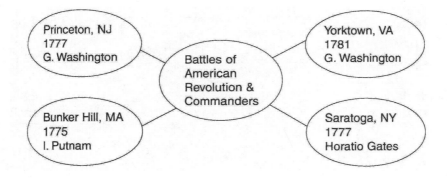

FLOW CHARTS AND TIME LINES

Like a concept map, a flow chart shows the relationship between related ideas. The flow chart works particularly well when you are working with data that has some type of sequence such as the development of a cell during meioses or the chronology of events or dates for battles during the Civil War. (**See FIGURE 5-4a**) A flow chart's value is that it can connect dates and times to events. It can also provide an effective way to summarize and put into your own words the significant data concerning each milestone.

Time lines also organize material that occurs chronologically. A time line can be used to show the order and length of time in which historical events follow. Time lines can be simple and just point out the time of the event or they can be more elaborate and give facts and examples about the occurrence.

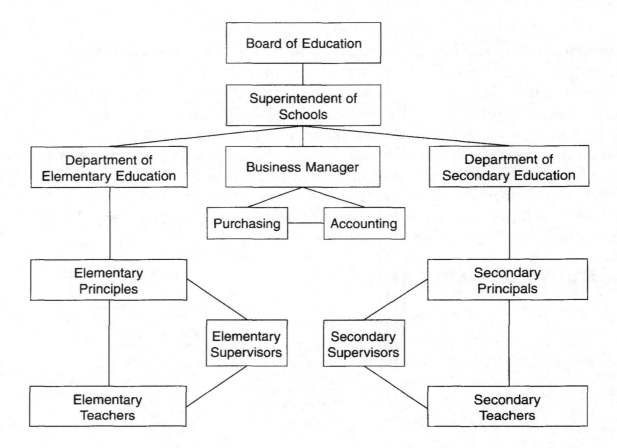

FIGURE 5-4 A & B EXAMPLES OF A FLOW CHART AND TIME LINES

a.   A flow chart showing the typical organization of a small school district.
b.   Simple time line:

Socrates	Plato	Aristotle	Cicero	Aquinas
469–399 B.C.	427–322 B.C.	384–322 B.C.	106–43 B.C.	1225–1274 A.D.

More elaborate time line:

Socrates	Plato	Aristotle
469–399 B.C.	427–322 B.C.	384–322 B.C.
Greek Idealism,	Greek idealist,	Greek Realist
Political conservativism	Classification of humans by intellectual abilities	Education based on classical Realism

KEEP A DAILY/WEEKLY PLANNER

Writing things down is, of course, the safest way to remember material you want to keep for a long time. A daily/weekly planner can be a place where a student keeps their most important information. It can be used to keep schedules for classes and meetings, the names of classmates and professors and study times. It can also be used to remind us of things that need to be accomplished in the future like a big exam or a major term paper.

You can find planners that display a day at a time, a week at a time or even a month at a time. We have found that a planner that displays a week at a time is the most efficient. It allows the student to know what important events are coming up during that week at a single glance and to plan accordingly. It also helps to find a planner that displays the days of that month and the days of the following month (**See FIGURE 5-5**). If you have the days of the month displayed, you can circle dates in the future that are important, so that you can page forward to see what needs to be done.

The planner can also be used to increase your vocabulary by having a 'new word a day' section. There are several commercial packages that provide a new word per day. However, it is just as effective to set up your own vocabulary building program, particularly if you are using vocabulary that is taken from the college classes you are enrolled in at the time. This is easy to set up by checking the class's syllabus for the dates you will be going over certain chapters in a textbook. Then use the vocabulary lists from each chapter to set up your program. Remember to schedule the words that you are learning prior to the time you begin the chapter including those words in class. This technique will allow you to review and practice new vocabulary at any spare moment.

A planner can be a very valuable tool to you, but its effectiveness is dependent on your effort to use it consistently and to maintain and keep current each area. As in everything, it takes practice and time to develop your ideal planner.

FIGURE 5-5   A PAGE FROM A WEEKLY PLANNER

Sept-95						
S	M	T	W	TH	F	S
					1	2
3	4	5	6	7	8	9
10	11	12	13	14	15	16
17	18	19	20	21	22	23
24	25	26	27	28	29	30

Oct-95						
S	M	T	W	TH	F	S
1	2	3	4	5	6	7
8	9	10	11	12	13	14
15	16	17	18	19	20	21
22	23	24	25	26	27	28
29	30	31				

Monday, Sept 4

7: _____

_____

8: John for breakfast _____

_____

9: study _____

_____

10: study _____

_____

11: _____

_____

12: psych class-group project due __

_____

1: _____

_____

2. Meet Al at gym _____

_____

3: _____

_____

4: study _____

_____

5: study _____

_____

6: _____

_____

Evening: Meet study group for 10-15-95 test 7:30 PM @ Col. Lib. _____

_____

_____

_____

Use Association

Another way to improve your memory is to use associations. When you use this technique, you are trying to link new information to facts you have learned in the past. When we associate new material to already processed information, it helps to strengthen our ability to retrieve it from memory. The reason that it works, is that by associating new ideas to old information, we are better able to put it into a context that is familiar. Therefore, we are not trying to remember an isolated act but are simply adding a new item into an already existing body of knowledge. For example, what if you were trying to remember two lists of ten words and the first list was made up of nonsense words like *KERJUP* or *SEMPOG* while the second list of words was made up of English words such as *STREET* or *FATHER*. For most English speaking people, the second list would be much easier to memorize because they could associate these words to something they already know.

Association can also be used to help memory, by putting groups of facts into packets of information.

Mnemonic Devices

Mnemonic devices are devices that help the memory remember or retrieve information. These techniques can be very helpful when students are trying to remember lists of things or are trying to recreate a series or sequence of events. Although mnemonic devices can help you bring back facts or allow you to retrieve words in a certain order, there are some draw backs that may hinder the learning process. A few of these problem areas are listed below.

1. These devices do not insure that you will understand the material you are trying to bring back. To understand, you must have other connections or associations that will relate the new information to a larger body of knowledge.
2. Some mnemonic devices can be very difficult to remember. There are some pegging systems which we will discuss later in the chapter which require the student to remember dozens of different questions. Therefore, the mnemonic device may be as hard to learn as the material from your course. However, once you have learned the system, you can use it over and over again.
3. Some mnemonic systems can at times confuse the student. If a system is not thoroughly learned or hasn't been used for a long time, it can sometimes

throw the student off. If they become dependant on the system and the system fails, which it can when under pressure of an exam, then the student could be in for a long day.

Even though there are some drawbacks in using mnemonic devices, they can still be a valuable tool if they are used correctly. The following is a list of devices that can be used and some suggestions for how to use them.

ACRONYMS

An acronym is a word made up of letters that indicate a series of other words. For example, if you were trying to remember the names of the five Great Lakes in the United States, you could use the acronym **HOMES**:

H uron
O ntario
M ichigan
E rie
S uperior

Each letter in the word represents the beginning letter in one of the five Great Lakes. Acronyms are good to use if you need to remember lists of things like a series of names or a list of events. You should try to keep the acronym under seven letters particularly if you are making up nonsense words as an acronym. If the acronym becomes too long, there is a chance you will not remember it.

SENTENCES

Very similar to the method of using acronyms is using an original or nonsense sentence to give you clues to a list or sequence of information. Instead of using a single word (acronym) to indicate the beginning letter of a series of facts that you would like to remember, you can use sentences to do the same thing. For example, if you wanted to remember all the classifications of animals in Biology you might use the following sentence.

Figure 5.6 **King Phillip Came Over For Gin and Soda.**

K ingdon
P hylum
C lass
O rder
F amily
G enus
S pecies

The first letter in each word in the sentence indicates a first letter in the material you want to learn. The advantage to using sentences rather than acronyms is that you can use longer lists of information. Even when the sentence is silly, there is an association between the words which makes it easier to remember.

One problem that can occur is that you make the sentence too long and silly. For instance, what if you used the sentence: Tom Munster Asked Sharon If Games Indeed Industrialized Indian Identity which Reaches Confusing Ideas and Images about Generous but Strange Illusions Daily? This sentence, which gives clues to the Erikson's eight stages of personality
development, is so confusing and without any real association that it can be counterproductive. You waste your time trying to memorize something which is more difficult than the material you were trying to learn in the first place. You should try to make your sentences simple and they should make some sense even if they are silly. To make a long non-associated sentence defeats the purpose of this mnemonic device.

RHYMES

Rhymes can be of some help with short memory sequences. However, most of the time, it is easier to remember the material than to try to find rhymes which will help you to remember specific facts. If some bit of information fits easily into a rhyme, then use it. It will be easier to recall the information, just try to make sure that creating a rhyme is not more of a problem than an advantage. (see FIGURE 5-7)

FIGURE 5-7 USING RHYMES FOR MEMORIZATION

Thirty days hath September, April, June and November

All the rest have thirty-one

Twenty-eight and February's done

Pegging Systems

Pegging systems can be simple or complex. Pegging systems work on the same basis as was discussed earlier in the chapter. Pegging works on the principle of organization, association and visualization. You can set up a series of words that can be memorized, such as (**See FIGURE 5-7**):

FIGURE 5-8 AN EXAMPLE OF A PEGGING SYSTEM

1. One is bun
2. Two is a shoe
3. Three is a tree
4. Four is a door
5. Five is a hive
6. Six is a stick
7. Seven is heaven
8. Eight is a gate
9. Nine is a line
10. Ten is a hen

This pegging system is organized around the numbers 1—10. The numbers are then associated to an object or place by using a rhyme, such as the pairs used in **FIGURE 5-7**. This visualization is used to link any list of information to objects in the pegging system. For example, if we wanted to learn a list of books that are important to American literature, we might link them like this:

The Old Man and the Sea paired with a bun. I may visualize an old man sailing on a giant bun in a choppy sea. Once I have made the connection "bun" and Old Man and the Sea, I have a strong visual picture, which I can now also relate to a place in order, (bun is one). Sometimes, it also helps to make visualizations which are different or funny. For most people this helps the storage and retrieval of information from memory. Pegging systems can be simple or complex. In the one mentioned earlier, the student had to learn ten number-object associations. Therefore, he or she could only connect ten pieces of information to this particular pegging system. However, there are many other systems which are much more complex in which a list of hundreds of items are possible.

You can also create your own pegging system by using a series of objects that are familiar to you. In this case, you will not have to memorize a standard pegging system. The objects you choose will be easier to recall because they have a personal association. For example, you could develop a system of pegs that are based on furniture or things in your own bedroom. You know the order of objects in your room, i.e.

As you walk through your bedroom door there is a **dresser** on the left

Going clockwise you have a large **chair**

Continuing going clockwise there is your **television**

Continuing on is your **bed**

Finishing the layout of your bedroom is a **fish tank**

Each position in your room acts as a peg. This is an easy and quick system because you probably don't have to memorize the order of the objects in your room. Therefore, you will have created an organization for your system. Second, because you are already familiar with each item in your room you will be able to have a strong visual picture of them in your head. Once you have created an organization with a visual reference all you need to do is associate whatever list of things you're trying to learn with an object in your system. For example, just as we linked a book's title to an object in the first pegging system we discussed, you can link a book's title to an object in your pegging system based on the objects in your room.

Mnemonic devices can be helpful for storing and retrieving information from memory, but they are only a tool. They can not solve all memory problems. The best way is to begin a program using some of the techniques mentioned in this chapter. Try to be consistent and try not to give up. You can improve your memory if you give yourself a chance.

EXERCISES CHAPTER FIVE

Exercise 5-1 Stages of memory

Instructions: Name two characteristics that are typical of each of the three stages of memory.

    A.   Sensory memory

        1. _____

            _____

        2. _____

            _____

    B. Short-term memory

        1. _____

            _____

        2. _____

            _____

    C. Long-term memory

        1. _____

            _____

Exercise 5-2 Draw a concept map

Instructions: Draw a concept map that depicts long-term memory.

Exercise 5-3   Create a day/week planner

Instructions: Using the planner below, create a typical day during the semester. Remember to use the monthly calendars to show important dates in the future.

```
         Sept-95                            Oct-95
  S   M   T   W  TH  F   S          S   M   T   W  TH  F   S
                      1   2          1   2   3   4   5   6   7
  3   4   5   6   7   8   9          8   9  10  11  12  13  14
 10  11  12  13  14  15  16         15  16  17  18  19  20  21
 17  18  19  20  21  22  23         22  23  24  25  26  27  28
 24  25  26  27  28  29  30         29  30  31
```

Monday, Sept 4

7: _____   1: _____
   _____   _____
8: _____   2: _____
   _____   _____
9: _____   3: _____
   _____   _____
10: _____   4: _____
   _____   _____
11: _____   5: _____
   _____   _____
12: _____   6: _____
   _____
   _____
_____
_____
_____
_____

119

Exercise 5-4 Write an Acronym that Helps You on the Next Test

Instructions: Try to write an acronym for your favorite song/album and music group.

1. _____

   _____

2. _____

   _____

Exercise 5-5 Create a Sentence That Help You Remember a List

Instructions: Create two sentences that will help you remember a list of facts that you want to bring back.

a. _____

   _____

b. _____

   _____

Technology in the College Classroom

Introduction | In this chapter, you will use techniques that help you get the most out of the technology that is part of the modern college classroom. You will also learn how to use library databases and the basic steps in researching and documenting a paper. You will review the policy on plagiarism. If you are considering a distance education course, this chapter will give you hints that will help you succeed.

Goals | After you have completed the work in the chapter you will:

- Maximize learning from video, PowerPoint and other technical presentations.
- Navigate the library databases as you research a paper.
- Appreciate the importance of academic honesty in your work.
- Make an informed decision about distance education courses.
- Confidently express your own opinion of the essay.

Activities/Tasks | These are the steps you need to take to complete the activities/tasks in the chapter. You should check off as you complete each one.

1. Prepare and use a format for taking notes from PowerPoint_____
2. Complete a search of at least two databases _____
3. Put two references into APA format_____
4. Find the college's policy on plagiarism and academic honesty____
5. View an online course (ask a professor or student to see theirs) and write a reaction paper (Action)_____
6. Read and complete a summary of the assigned essay._____
7. Answer or add at least one general knowledge question._____

You will:

1. Demonstrate in class the notes you took during a PowerPoint lesson and describe techniques that you used.
2. Write and submit a report on the searches you did on two databases, giving a least two titles of articles from each database.
3. Using two of the articles you found in the database search, put two of the references into APA format. Submit the references to your instructor.
4. Participate in a class discussion about plagiarism and academic honesty.
5. Write a reaction paper (at least three paragraphs) on the online course you previewed. Give the subject of the course, what you liked about the course and what you did not like about the course.
6. Write and submit an essay on the critical thinking exercise, incorporating your developed skills and the new one (summarizing) in this chapter.
7. Contribute to the general knowledge fund.

Chapter Six: Technology in the College Classroom

The use of computers, databases, and other technology is a large and growing component of the modem college classroom. Some professors use presentation programs (PowerPoint®) to deliver the course material instead of writing on the board. Some classes are "hybrid" classes meaning that a large portion of the course is conducted online, using course software such as WebCt®, First Class®, and Blackboard®. The rest of the course meets on a regular basis on campus. Finally, some courses are taught completely online. All communication and testing are done through the course software. Generally, there are no in class meetings; however, some professors require on-campus or on-site test sessions. You should inquire if you will need to come on campus or arrange for a test site before you enroll in a distance education or online course. The modern library provides access to databases, which are electronic catalogs of books, articles and other resource material. Using a database is the new way to research information for a paper. This chapter introduces you to some of these new trends and capabilities in technology.

TAKING ADVANTAGE OF POWERPOINT® PRESENTATIONS

At first glance, following a PowerPoint® slide presentation that contains course information seems an easy and helpful way to get the course content. If the professor hands out the presentation to you, you may feel that all note taking is done. That assumption would not be accurate; you still need to work with and process the material in the presentation. A few suggestions on how to use these presentations to your benefit and a few cautions about them are given.

1. The PowerPoint® slides do provide an outline of the course content but the commentary of the professor should have your attention. Take notes on what is being said. Do not spend the time copying the slides. You can design a format for this process, similar to the one below.
    a. Write down the <u>title</u> of the slide.

<u>Title of Slide</u>: *Factors in Memory Retrieval*

b. Focus on the professor's comments. When a statement is made that includes information on the slide, get the statement into your notes. Put a mark (plus sign, a star, or a P) next to the statement. This will remind you that this is important information: it's in both the presentation and the professor's lecture.

FIGURE 6.1 **FORMAT FOR NOTETAKING FROMPOWERPOINT.®**

Slide	Professor's Comments
Serial Position Effect (fill this in after you've listened to the professor's comment)	Remembering a list/more likely to remember the first and last items/called serial position effect.++
State-dependent memory (fill this in after you've listened to the professor's comments)	More likely to remember information when in the same place as when you learned it. ++

c. When you review your notes after class, you can fill in the "slide" portion.

2. If you are given a paper copy of the PowerPoint®, you should again focus on the lecture. Usually there is space next to the slide to take notes. You can use this space during class but remember to transfer the information to your notebook or class binder. It is important that you work with and process the class session material.

WAYS TO SUCCEED IN A DISTANCE EDUCATION COURSE

Studying for a distance education course is similar to studying for a traditional course, with a few important differences. Here are some suggestions; not all will be for you, so choose ones that make sense for your particular situation.

TIME MANAGEMENT

Most students who take an online course are attracted by the amount of time—in travel and classroom time—that can be saved by logging on to their home computers to do the work. Yes, time is saved in the direct teaching of the material; however, extra time needs to be spent in learning (or self-teaching) the material. It is, therefore, extremely important that you make a REASONABLE schedule that you can stick to.

A reasonable schedule includes reading and study time as well as time for daily activities, such as work, eating, errands, rest, and relaxation. A general rule of thumb is that for every hour spent in the classroom, at least two hours should be spent in learning the material. So, set aside three hours per week to read and take notes on the text and course information and an additional six hours to learn the material and complete the assignments.

NOTE-TAKING

You will need to take a lot of notes, perhaps more than in a traditional class. To make your notes help you, you can try the following techniques. (See Chapter 3 for more detail.)

1. Get a 2- or 3- ring binder and holed paper.
2. Take notes on only one side of the page. You can easily rearrange your notes when preparing for the essay exams. For example, if you are asked to compare the theories of Erikson and Freud, you can pull these pages out of the binder and work with them as you study.
3. Draw a line down the page about 2½ inches from the margin. Write notes on the material on the space to the right of this line. A few hours later or the next day, read your notes and put the main ideas or most important terms in the space to the left of the line (the recall column). You might want to use a different colored pen to highlight the main ideas or terms. You can also add ideas and related concepts in the recall column as you move deeper into the course. You may pick up ideas from classmates as you communicate in the forums and e-mail.
4. When you return to your notes, cover the detailed notes with a piece of paper. Look at the recall column and recite (Yes, speak out loud!) a brief version of the detailed notes.

This process of a) active reading and writing; b) summarizing the material; and C) speaking the material is powerful because it involves you with the material in three different ways. Practice makes perfect!

TEXTBOOK READING

Textbook publishers spend a lot of time (and you spend a lot of money) on organizing and printing their books in ways designed to support learning. Here are some ideas that may help your textbook work for you. (See Chapter 2 for additional tactics.)

1. Glance through the chapter before you begin reading. You will see chapter objectives and topic headings listed, usually in a different color type. These are the important topics in the chapter. Take a few minutes to ask yourself what you already know about these topics.

2. Decide how many pages or sections you plan to do at this session. It sounds wonderful to say "I'm going to read and outline four chapters" but not very realistic. Even if you manage to turn all the pages, the human attention span rarely allows this time to be productive. You can estimate your attention span by beginning to read the textbook and timing how long it is before your mind begins to wander. Once you realize that you are no longer reading productively, count the number of words you have read. Now do the same exercise after you have done some of the following warm-up activities.

A. Creating Advance Organizers:

- Count the number of pages in the chapter. An average beginning reading speed is about two pages in five minutes. If the chapter has 20 pages, it will take about 50 minutes to just read the material. If the material is brand new to you or extra difficult, it may take longer to read. The first thing to do is plan for these fifty minutes.
- The human mind remembers best in "chunks." It is sensible to now divide the chapter into major topics; here's where the topic headings come in handy. Plan to read one topic at a time, marking or making notations in the book (see below) as you read.

B. Review and Recite:

- At the end of each section, review and recite what you have read. If you can't remember, go back and re-read that section. You also might want to take a break if this happens repeatedly. Go on to the next section. When you've finished with the amount of pages or sections you planned, ask yourself "What did I learn?"

- You can take notes on the material as you read but read the topic or section before you start taking notes. There is much repetition in a textbook; when you've read through the topic you can see the new material you need to take notes on and not waste your time writing unnecessary notes. Don't copy the textbook; you should put the information into your own words, preserving the important terms and vocabulary.

C. Marking the Textbook:

- Read with a pencil. An efficient way to cover textbook material is to mark the important terms, ideas and concepts in the book. Do not get in the habit of dragging a highlighter along the line as you read. Not everything is of equal importance. If you need a highlight to remind you that, in fact, you have read a particular page or section, go back to B above.
- Leave notes to yourself and ask yourself questions. Hopefully, as you read psychology, questions will arise about how this idea might apply to you and your life. "Is this why Cousin P acts the way he does?" Making a note in the text will reinforce the application of the material. Also, put ???? next to portions that you do not understand so you can find the answers later or in another place.
- Use the wide margin on the page for notes and connections between terms. Circle important terms and make connecting lines and arrows. Whatever triggers your memory can be used to support your learning.
- If the idea of writing in the book really bothers you, get a supply of post-it notes. They come in all sizes and colors. Write on the post-it and leave them on the pages in place of pencil notes.

Learning Styles

Not all of us learn in the same way. Many people are visual learners and gain most of the information through reading. Other people are iconic learners and find graphs and charts very helpful. If you are an auditory learner, you might do well to tape record the important information and play it back while driving to and from work. If you are a tactile learner, using your hands to create your own graphs and diagrams, design a demonstration and explore the Internet for good Psychology sites will be a satisfying way to learn.

Whatever your personal style, it will be necessary to become comfortable with the other kinds. If you prefer to read the book and skip the graphs, force yourself to de-code a graph. Graphs convey a lot of information in a condensed way. You will need to develop some skill in tactile learning in order to do the course.

Another dimension of learning style concerns how social you are while you learn. If you are an individual learner, distance education courses may be just right for you. Remember, however, that when you are in a traditional class you cannot help but hear and see other students. This source of input is not as easily available in a distance education class. If you are a group learner, you might feel isolated at first. It will be important for both the individual learner and the group learner to make contact with others in the course through the bulletin board and e-mail.

And, finally, each of us likes to be closer to or farther away from the instructor. If you like personal, face-to-face interaction you need to take steps to keep in contact with the instructor. You can do this easily by e-mail or drop by during office hours to chat. Another way to have this type of interaction is to share what you are studying with family and friends. Many activities in the textbook or on the Web ask you to include friends in gathering the information.

Stay Curious

Not every topic will be of equal interest to you but if you try to apply what you are studying to the reading you do, the TV and movies you see, and observations you make of daily life, you should see the value in what you are studying. Keep a list of real events that you encounter that relate to the topics in the course. Post the interesting ones to the entire class on the bulletin board.

Researching and Writing a Paper

In many courses, you will be required to write a research paper. This means you will need to find information to use in your paper. You will need to give references, in a standard format, to document your sources and, importantly, to avoid the occurrence of plagiarism. This section introduces you to research resources that help you locate, evaluate, take notes on information, write and document your paper.

The professor goes through the syllabus on the first day of class and mentions that a research paper is due on week 13 of the course. That seems like a long way off but, to do a good job on the paper, you will need to plan a schedule to get the paper done. Probably the best way to do this is to start at the end. If the paper is due December 1, plot out what needs to be done by the middle of November, and the last week of October, etc. Take a look at Figure 6.2 for some ideas.

FIGURE 6.2 TIMELINE FOR RESEARCH PAPER.

December 1	Turn in final paper.
November 14	Type first draft.
November 10	Organize and write first draft.
November 1	Complete research/index cards.
October 5	Decide on research articles, books, etc.
October 1	Get topic approval
September 15	Visit library and search databases. Select topic.

EXPLORE

Once you have a schedule in place, begin to think about possible topics. Your first task is to narrow the subject of your paper to two or three topics. Your professor may have given you a list to choose from; if not, use your course textbook to give you an idea or two. You can look at the table of contents and the index for topics. Try to find something that interests you and is related to the course. For example, if you are interested in fashion and you are in an American history course, you might do a paper on how women's fashion changes according to historical events. Clothes during World War II (in the 1940's) used less fabric because fabric production was needed for soldiers' uniforms. If you are a music fan, and in a psychology course, you could write a paper on the impact of fame and celebrity on a person's ego or sense of self. Your paper will be better and more enjoyable if you find a topic that interests you.

FIND

Once you've thought about a few possibilities, visit the library. Ask the librarian to show you how to search the databases if you do not know how to do so already. If you can put your idea in the form of a question that your paper wants to answer, you will be able to use the vast of amount of information found in the databases. Using the ideas above, the question for the first example would be "what influence did World War II have on women's fashion? Why is this the case?" When you put the key terms fashion and World War II into the database, all the articles on this subject will appear for you to review.

A database is a digital collection of articles and books on a particular area. The chart below lists the major databases available at most community colleges.

FIGURE 6.3 **TYPICAL DATABASES AVAILABLE AT A COLLEGE LIBRARY.** (INFORMATION FROM LIBRARY HOMEPAGE AT ATLANTIC CAPE COMMUNITY COLLEGE AT HTTP://WWW.ATLANTIC.EDU).

Library Database Tutorials	Multimedia help with online research.
Library Book Catalog	Shows the collection of books in the college library.
netLibrary	Electronic books
EBSCOHost	Accesses Academic Search Premier; CINAHL and Health Source (nursing); Business Source Plus and more.
ScienceDirect	Over 2 million peer reviewed in the sciences, arts, humanities, business, psychology and sociology.
Literature Resource Center	Critical information on 120,000 authors and their works.
Lexis-Nexus	News, legal, business and medical information from thousands of full-text publications.
ERIC	Education abstracts from professional publications.

DECIDE

At this stage, it is a good idea to talk to your professor about your topic. Once you have his or her approval, you can begin to seriously research your topic.

RESEARCH

Your task now is to begin your research; this means finding articles or books and other sources of information on your topic. The librarian can help you with the databases. Some databases allow you to print the full article; other databases give you only the reference (where you can find the article). You can order an article that you think will be helpful using an "interlibrary loan." Libraries share information and will send a copy of an article or book when it is requested by another library.

Perhaps the most important part of research is to evaluate the quality of the information. Avoid the Web as a major source of material. The material there may or may not be accurate. It is often someone's opinion or personal experience. Not all articles, books and sources are of equal caliber. Look for professional articles and sources. One type of article is called "peer reviewed;" these are articles that are reviewed before they are published by authorities in the area of study. Use the check list below to evaluate the articles, books and sources.

- What are the author(s)'s credentials?
- Are the authors affiliated with a university, college or institute?
- Are there any other articles by the author(s)?
- Is the article referenced with other sources?
- What types of statistics are used? (Number of subjects etc.)
- Is the article peer reviewed and in a professional journal?
- What is the date of publication? (Usually your references should be no older than 10 years. You may use older references from major theorists and historical documents.)

TAKE NOTES

After you have found some articles or books, you can begin to take notes. Now is a good time to outline your paper. (See outline format below.)

Index cards can be helpful now. Make a list of all your references and number them. As you read the article or book, keep notes on what you read, putting on the note index card the number of the reference you are using; also include the page number. Keep track of all the information you put into your notes. You can also indicate on the index card what point the information supports. When you are ready to write, put all the cards supporting a point in one pile. You are now ready to write a first draft.

FIGURE 6.4 **APA (AMERICAN PSYCHOLOGICAL ASSOCIATION) SIMPLIFIED FORMAT**

<u>Introduction</u>

Write down your thesis or main idea in your section.

<u>Idea 1</u>: Put the heading for this section to the left and underline it.

Point A.

Point B.

<u>Idea 2</u>: Put the heading for this section to the left and underline it.

Point A.

Point B.

<u>Conclusion</u>

CITING AND REFERENCING

When you use the ideas of another person in your writing, you must give credit to that author. In a psychology or sociology paper, you need to use the American Psychology Association (APA) style of referencing. If you do not properly reference your work, your professor may reject the paper because of plagiarism. In repeat cases of plagiarism, a student may be expelled from the college. You should become familiar with the college policy on plagiarism.

When you quote part of the article directly (word-for-word), you need to put the author(s) name and date of publication and the page number in the narrative of your work.

FIGURE 6.5 **SAMPLE CITATION IN THE TEXT**

> Trait theories attempt to "explain personality and differences between people in terms of personal characteristics that are stable across situations" (Wood, S., Wood, E. & Boyd, 2003, p. 322).

If you are paraphrasing an idea — in other words putting it into your own words — use the above style but do not include the page numbers. Look in your textbook for other examples.

At the end of your paper, you will need to put all your references into a reference list. Going in alphabetical order, show the author, date, title (underlined or italicized) city of publication and the publisher of each book. For an article, include the author, date, title (underlined or italicized), journal, volume number and the page numbers. Look in your textbook for examples of citing and referencing (at the end of the book). There is an information literacy tutorial on the college homepage at http://www.atlantic.edu.

FIGURE 6.6 **SAMPLE REFERENCES**

From a journal:

Sokolov, E.N. (2000). Perception and the conditioning reflex. *International Journal of Psychophysiology*, 35, 197–217.

From a book:

Spearman, G. (1927). The abilities of man. New York: Macmillan.

From an electronic source:

Quinn, T. The global HIV/AIDS pandemic 2002: A status report. The Hopkins HIV report [September 2002 online edition]. Retrieved December 28, 2002. From http://hopkins-aids.edu.

RE-WRITE AND COMPLETE

It is a rare paper that is polished after the first draft. Leave enough time to let the paper "sit" for a few days. Return to the paper and carefully re-read it. Check for grammar and spelling. Add a title page with the title, course, professor's name, and date. Do not add a picture to the title page unless advised to do so. You should also do an abstract that gives a brief summary of the paper and what you concluded. Check that all your references are included (in alphabetical order) in the list and attach as the final page or pages of your paper.

PAT YOURSELF ON THE BACK

If you follow these suggestions, it will be apparent to your professor that you have tried to do a good job on the assignment. Organization, neatness, good research and referencing will add to the quality of the work. Leave yourself enough time to do all these steps and you are on your way to a successful paper.

Exercise 3: Putting References into APA format.

Use the index cards below to put two sources that you found in exercise 1 into the proper reference format. See the samples in the chapter.

Card 1

Card 2

PART II

Part 2: Critical Thinking Modules

Module	Title	Page	Skill
1	Scenarios		Clarify information by being objective.
2	Topic Sentence		Finding main point of paragraph/Topic sentence.
3	"On Kids and Slasher Movies"		Find controlling idea, give general summary.
4	"The Failure of Feminism"		Find controlling idea; give direct support.
5	"Ambivalence of Abortion"		Find general conflict.
6	"The Gap Between Gay & Straight"		Find general conflict with direct support.
7	"Who's Afraid of the Big Bad Bang"		Find author's view of conflict.
8	"On Becoming a Chicano"		Find persuasive techniques used by author.
9	"A Political Correction"		Give personal opinion on the conflict.
10	Districting by Pigmentation		Analyze others' view of the conflict.
11	"The Melting Pot Is Still Simmering"		Give personal opinion of the conflict & support with parallel evidence.
12	"The Myth of Classlessness"		Give personal opinion and another perspective.
13	Library Assignment		Find controversial articles in today's news and analyze according to skills from previous modules.

MODULE #1

Objectives:

1. Students will gain a basic understanding of the principles related to Critical Thinking.
2. Students will be able to identify the four basic approaches needed to clarify or substantiate information.
3. Students will begin to use critical thinking skills to solve problems in their every day life.
4. Students will begin to develop a more extensive vocabulary by building a Flashcard File.

Assignments:

A. Read INTRODUCTION TO CRITICAL THINKING..
B. Complete Exercise #1, Questions 1 – 8.
C. Flashcard File

Instructions:

1. Use a 3" x 5" index card.
2. Find at least three words from the reading assignment that you did not know or were unsure of the usage.
3. On the front of the index card print the new word.
   Turmoil
4. On the back of the index card, write the word's definition. Omit the word in the definition
   Definition: Commotion; Trouble; agitation Sentence: After John broke up with Sally, her Emotions were in
5. Also on the back of the index card, use the word in a sentence. Replace the word with a blank.

There is a difference between knowing and understanding. You can know a lot about something and not really understand it.

*Charles F. Kettering

INTRODUCTION: WHAT IS CRITICAL THINKING?

There are many different definitions of critical thinking. One definition is offered by Anita Woolfolk in her book Educational Psychology 5th Ed. (1 993).[1] Critical thinking is "evaluating conclusions by logically and systematically examining the problem, the evidence, and the solutions." A second definition of critical thinking is given to us by Linda Elder and Richard Paul from the Foundation of Critical Thinking, Santa Clara, California. They state "critical thinking is that mode of thinking about any subject, content, or problem in which the thinker improves the quality of his or her thinking by skillfully taking charge of the structures inherent in thinking and imposing intellectual standards upon them."[2]

Although these definitions may sound complicated or appear to have little to do with how a person deals with everyday life, there are some practical and fairly simple ways we can go about understanding what critical thinking means and how it can be important to our lives. First, we think and make choices, decisions and judgments about our lives and the things that go on around us all the time. We choose the clothes we wear, what TV programs we want to watch, how to spend our money and raise our kids. We make hundreds of decisions each day. Certainly some of these choices are more difficult and more important than others. But do we know how or why we make these decisions? Do we even know how these choices affect our lives?

So, for the purposes of this course, we are going to consider critical thinking as a process where we make a conscious effort to:
1. check if the information we are getting is objective and reliable, which means is the information we are using proven facts or just opinions;
2. determine if the information may be clouded by emotion or prejudice;
3. inspect the information to see if all the evidence necessary for making a decision is being offered and;
4. make sure that information appears logical and consistent with the conclusions that are being drawn.

---

[1] Woolfolk, A (1993). Educational Psychology, 5th Ed. NY Allyn & Bacon.
[2] Paul, R. & Elder, J. (1999) The Miniature Guide to Critical Thinking,

WHY IS CRITICAL THINKING IMPORTANT?

Today's world can be a confusing and frightening place. Things that were taken for granted just a few years in the past seem to be ancient history. Technology, society, even our families are changing so quickly it's difficult to make any sense out of it. Adding to the confusion is the amount of information that is heaped on us each day by the media, our jobs and even by our friends and relatives. Much of this information can be confusing or conflicting. So how do we handle all this **turmoil**?

Turmoil
trouble

Concepts & Tools. CA: The Foundation for Critical Thinking.

People deal with these problems in many different ways. However, there seems to be two major categories for solving the problems associated with modern society. The first way is to limit much of the information coming in whether it seems reasonable or not. We can limit this information in a number of ways. We can just ignore its meaning or consequence. We can chose to believe only the information we like or have always believed or we can choose bits and pieces of information that do not upset us. Handling information in this way can be both dangerous and self-defeating. The person who denies that smoking cigarettes is damaging their health, obviously is not objectively processing the information. The person who continues to drive a car after drinking alcohol, is not being reasonable.

Unrelenting
Not giving in

Another way to control the hectic **unrelenting** pace of today's world is to begin to make decisions and judgments based on fact and on objective **assessments** of the situation. When you make a reasonable judgment, you will have an opportunity to predict the outcome of your actions. This is not to say that you will always be correct or that your expectations will be met, but it will allow you to be more in control of your future. The ability to understand what you are doing today will help you adjust to your future.

Assessment
judgment

The process of beginning to consider the options that come into your life is not easy. We have all taken so many things for granted for so long that it is difficult to make decisions about how we live. But there is a way to get some control over your life. If you take a risk and begin to think critically, you have a chance to direct your own future.

Critical thinking is not generally taught in schools. Much of education is educated to either teaching fundamental skills such as reading and mathematics or to acquiring facts and information about particular disciplines such as history and science. These areas are all important, but they do not necessarily prepare you to adjust your thinking, make choices, question positions or to take a number of different perspectives on the same issue. Many times people are taught not to question, but to accept facts and information as they are presented. As we look back in time, we know that things change. John Stuart Mill once wrote "(t)hat which seems the height of mod absurdity in one generation often becomes the height of wisdom in the next." e What was once a fact is now no longer a viable or reasonable answer. During Christopher Columbus's time, it was thought the world was, in fact, flat. Today, it sounds ridiculous that someone could believe the world was flat, but to the average Fourteen Century person that was simple common sense.

Credibility
believability

Critical thinking gives us techniques and strategies to take the growing amount of often conflicting facts and information and make sound judgments and draw conclusions on how to use the facts in our lives. It gives us a way to examine our world and make decisions based on **credible**, objective, and logical thinking.

HOW DO YOU BECOME A CRITICAL THINKER?

You might now see that critical thinking may have its uses, but how do you acquire strong critical thinking skills. Like everything else you learn, you have to work at it. Thinking skills can be practiced and improved over time, but not without effort. The more you try to use critical thinking the better you will become at it. You begin with the easier skills and progress onto the more complicated ones. In this book we are going to base some of our progression of thinking skills on Bloom's Taxonomy. (See pages) This taxonomy is a **hierarchy** of thinking beginning with the accumulation of information or knowledge and onto the more complex thinking skills of synthesis and critical evaluation. Each of these skills is important, but the later skills are more complicated and require lower skill acquisition before one becomes **adept** at them. This book is going to take you through the fundamentals of these skills by guiding you through a step by step process starting with the more simple concepts and ideas and moving progressively onward to the more complex. The book is organized into modules. Each module comes with a set of instructions and an exercise that will allow you to practice your skills at each level. As you get into the later modules, you will find the material becoming increasingly more complicated and possibly more difficult. You may need to spend more time on later modules and discuss strategies with classmates on how to complete the exercises.

Hierarchy
Skills in rank or order

Adept
skilled

We know what you have read about this book can sound ominous. However, it can also help you succeed in an increasingly confusing and complicated world. Success is a difficult thing to measure, but in the Words of Ralph Waldo Emerson, it can be achieved.

> *To laugh often and much; to win the respect of intelligent people and the affection of children; to earn the appreciation of honest critics and endure the betrayal of false friends; to appreciate beauty, to find the best in others; to leave the world a bit better, whether by a healthy child, a garden patch or a redeemed social condition; you know even one life has breathed easier because you have lived. This is to have succeeded.*

WHAT ARE PEOPLE REALLY SAYING?
FACT, FICTION OR SOMETHING IN BETWEEN?

If you can buy into the commitment of trying to use critical thinking as a means to understanding your world, then the next step is to begin to find a way to make your decisions more logical, more objective and more critical. The information given to us each day, whether it is verbal or written is not necessarily factual, objective or **unbiased**. Many times people will try to convince you that their point of view is the correct one. They may do this by making an argument for one side of an issue or another. For example, someone may try to convince you that a certain politician should be reelected for a political office. They may say things that they think you want to hear and link them to that particular politician:

Unbiased
Without
prejudice

"He/She is against raising taxes."
"He/She is out to help the little guy."
"He/She believes in God."

All of these statements are aimed at trying to persuade you to believe that this politician thinks and acts the same way you do. Because someone says that they believe one way or another does not mean that they behave consistently on that belief.

Substantiated
supported

The critical thinker is cautious about taking information that is not **substantiated**. The critical thinker begins to pose questions about the credibility of the statements; i.e., if the politician is against raising taxes, how has he/she voted in the past on tax issues? Are all tax raises against my own interest? Are there any other reasons that might influence why he/she does not want to raise taxes? On each of the above statements a number of questions could be asked. In the following exercise asks questions that might clarify the meaning of the speaker.

Exercise #1:

Directions: Read each of these scenarios. On a separate sheet of paper list at least three questions about each scenario and explain why these questions should be asked. Your questions should be directed at clarifying or substantiating the information given. Remember the four basic approaches that we discussed earlier in the manual:
- Is the information objective and reliable?
- Is the information free from bias or prejudice?
- Have all the facts necessary for making a decision been given?
- Are the conclusions warranted by the evidence?

1. A young man walks into a department store looking for a new pair of jeans. A sales clerk approaches and asks if he can help. The young

man describes what he wants and how much he wants to pay. The salesman says, "I have exactly what you want, except it costs a little bit more than you wanted to pay."

2. Chris and Sam are on their lunch break from work. Chris tells Sam about his date last night and how well he did sexually with her. Chris goes on and says that he does not want to go into the details, but he would be more than happy to get him a date with her.

3. Kelly and Jan are young teenage girls going to high school. Kelly invites Jan to come and spend a weekend at her parents' beach house. Bill, an older high school boy, is going to the beach on Saturday morning and she can get a ride with him. Kelly's parents will bring her home on Sunday.

4. Tom has saved up two thousand dollars from his job. He is looking for a place to invest the money so that he can buy a house someday. Hank, a good friend at work, tells Tom that his brother-in-law is starting out a new business and is looking for small investors. Hank is adamant that this is a 'no miss deal' and Tom should get into it immediately.

5. Eric saw Kathy coming out of the library with Alex. She was laughing and smiling. The next day Eric heard that Alex was going to ask Kathy out on a date. On the next night Kathy broke a date with Eric, because she said that she was not feeling well. Eric is considering breaking off his relationship with Kathy.

6. The advertisement said that you could lose up to 20 pounds in just two weeks. You could eat all of your favorite foods and it took very little will power. Brian was considering buying these weight loss pills because he wanted to look good for the summer.

7. When the supervisor arrived that afternoon twenty dollars was missing from the cash register. Bonnie was the last person at the register and just the other day she had been complaining about not having enough money to buy that new sweater. The supervisor was thinking about writing a letter to the manager accusing Bonnie of being a thief.

8. When John walked out of his apartment building he saw that his new ten-speed bike had been stolen. There had been two black kids sitting out front of his building when he came home this afternoon. He had known one of them and had heard that the kid was always in trouble. John was deciding whether he should call the police and tell them that his bike was stolen and that he thought he knew who did it.

MODULE #2

Objectives:

1. Students will determine the main or controlling idea when given a paragraph about a controversial issue.
2. Students will provide two sentences that support the main idea.
3. Students will add three new words to their Flashcard File.

Assignment:

Read THE SECOND STEP, in your manual.
Complete Exercise #2.
Add three new words to your Flashcard File. These words may come from the text or from another source.

Whatever you cannot understand, you cannot possess.

* Wolfgang Van Goethe

THE SECOND STEP

It is not always easy to understand what a person is trying to say especially when it is presented in written form. For the purposes of this course, most of your assignments will be given in written form, and your responses will also be in the form of an essay. However, you will have ample time during class discussions to talk about your assignments and to ask questions and make comments.

The exercise that you will be completing for this week's assignment deals with two of the fundamental skills that a reader needs to grasp when trying to understand an author's meaning. The first skill is finding the main or controlling idea of a paragraph. The main idea of a paragraph is generally contained in the topic sentence. This is the sentence about which the entire paragraph is going to be based. The topic sentence is usually the first sentence in the paragraph; however, it does not necessarily have to be the first. It could be the last sentence of the paragraph (which is another common place for it) or it could be in any other part of the paragraph. However, when trying to find the topic, the first place to look is the opening sentence. If it is not there, then look at the last sentence. Usually you will find it in one of these two places. For example, in the above paragraph, the topic sentence is the first one. It tells you what the rest of the paragraph is going to be about and that there are two skills that are going to be discussed. This sentence does not give you all the details about the paragraph, but it does give the controlling idea.

The second part of your assignment deals with identifying the details of the paragraph. Most paragraphs are going to be composed of detail sentences. The details are the supporting information. The details give the reader a more in-depth understanding of the top sentence. A few of the ways a detail sentence does this is by giving examples or by citing statistics or other information that might substantiate or clarify the topic sentence. In the exercise ahead there will be other types of supporting information. However, once you have figured out the topic sentence, you can be confident that the other sentences are there to support it.

Exercise #2

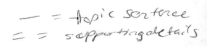

Instructions: On a separate sheet of paper identify the topic sentence of each of the following paragraphs. Then list two other sentences that support the topic sentence.

1. The long arm of racism still permeates our society. Twenty-one secret service agents stopped for breakfast at Denny's Restaurant. All but six were served in short order. The six were black. The restaurant chain faces a lawsuit in California based on a similar complaint from 32 black customers. (*New York Times*)

2. You've heard the numbers -10% of American men are gay, 2.7 million children are abused; one in eight women develops breast cancer. Politicians, activists, fund raisers, scientists and yes, magazine journalists routinely unload such staggering statistics on a trusting public. The numbers are presented as though they carry all the weight of scientific truth. Don't believe it. (*Time: April26, 1993*)

3. No parent wants to leave a child alone at home, but sometimes it's hard to avoid. Experts generally agree that no child under 10 should be left unsupervised, even for an hour. But even with older kids, "the choice should not be made lightly," warn child psychologists Lynette and Thomas Long. The child's maturity and the safety of the neighborhood should be carefully considered. (*Time: March 1, 1993*)

4. The assumption that dinosaurs were exothermic - cold blooded - was originally based on a simple argument. Reptiles are exothermic - they can't regulate their body heat. If they get too hot, they die. If they get too cold, they get sluggish. Dinosaurs were closely related to reptiles. End of argument. (*Time: April 26, 1990*)

5. Oh how we tried to rationalize it that night as the starting time for the movie came and went. My husband talked about his plans for a career change in the next year, to stem the staleness that fourteen years with the same investment-banking firm had brought him. A new baby would preclude that option. (*New York Time, 1976*)

6. Spring lures people outside, into the domain of the tick. And innumerable Lyme disease bearing ticks are still on the prowl. But doctors frequently

over-diagnose the disease, according to a study published last week in the Journal of the American Medical Association. The study shows that fewer than a quarter of patients referred to a Boston Lyme-disease clinic over a four-year period actually suffered actively from the disease. One problem, says the study, is that Lyme's flu like symptoms are similar to those of other maladies such as chronic fatigue syndrome. Despite the misdiagnoses, experts caution that the threat of infection is as strong as ever. (*US News& World Report:April 26, 1993*)

7. The 10,000 khaki-clad Afrikaner farmers were seething. Demonstrating under a Hot Transvaal sun in Potchefstroom last week, they shouted down a junior minister in President F. W. DeKlerk's cabinet when he rose to address them. Then they gave a standing ovation to retired South African Defense Force chief Constand Vijoen, who demanded a halt to DeKlerk's negotiations with the African National Congress and other parties. (*Time: May 17,1993*)

MODULE #3

Objectives:

1. Students will be able to read an article on a controversial issue and be able to describe the controlling idea.

2. Students will be able to write a brief summary of the article and be able to identify the author's reason or intent in writing the article.

3. Students will be able to pick out three new vocabulary words and be able to use them in a sentence.

Assignments:

1. Read the article "On Kids and Slasher Movies".
   a. Describe the article's controlling idea (why the author wrote the article)
   b. Summarize the article by selecting four major points that support the controlling idea within the article.
2. Find three new words from the text and use them in a sentence.

To him whose elastic and vigorous thought keeps pace with the sun, the day is a perpetual morning.

*Henry David Thoreau

ON KIDS AND SLASHER MOVIES
Michael Ventura

It's a simple thing, really, I shouldn't take it so seriously, I realize that. For its was only a child, a boy of about 10, buying a sinister evil toy, for Halloween. This was the toy:

Sininster
menacing

A **sinister** white mask and a quite convincing little meat cleaver, packaged together in cellophane. It's the "costume" of a maniac killer from one of the slasher movies. The boy wants to play at being a faceless, unstoppable murderer of innocent people (mostly women). At this moment, in this Woolworth's, that's this boy's idea of fun.

Understand that I didn't stand there and decide intellectually that this simple and small event is, when all is said and done, the worst thing I've seen. My body decided. My intestines, my knees, my chest. It was only later that I tried to think about it.

Fetish
Symbol of obsession

Allocating
distributing

This boy's eagerness to "play" maniac killer is an event worse than the Bomb, worse even than Auschwitz. Reduced to its simplest terms, the bomb is a **fetish**, an object of worship-like other objects of worship before it. It is used as an excuse for arranging the world in a certain fashion, **allocating** resources, assigning powers. It is insane, but in many ways it is an extension of familiar, even honored, insanities. As for the Nazi camps: The people being murdered knew, the camps became the measure of ultimate human evil. A crime to scar us all, and our descendants forever.

There is nothing so clear in the Woolworth's scene. The boy is certainly not committing a crime. The toy's merchandisers are within their rights. To legislate against them would be to endanger our freedoms. The mother buying the toy is perhaps making a mistake, perhaps not. Without knowing the boy, and knowing him well, who's to be certain that it isn't better for him to engage in, rather than repress, such play? The mother did not put the desire for the toy in him. Three thousand years of Judeo-Christian culture did that. Nor has the mother the power to take that desire from him. Nobody has that power. If he can want the toy at all, then it almost doesn't matter whether the toy exists or not. Doesn't the boy's need for such play exist with or without the toy?

Nor would I be too quick to blame the boy's desire on television and slasher films. The Nazis who crewed the camps and the scientists who built the bomb did not need television and slasher films to school them in horror. In fact, the worst **atrocities** from the pharaohs to Vietnam were committed quite ably before the first slasher film was made. Keeping your child away from TV may make you feel better, but can any child be protected from the total weight of Western history?

In a world shorn of order, stripped of traditions, molting every decade, every year, a dancing, varicolored snake of a century-pointless violence is evident everywhere, on every level. Professional soldiers are statistically safer than urban women; senseless destruction is visited on trees and on the ozone and on every species of life. No one feels safe anywhere. This has become the very meaning of 20th century.

So I am in a Woolworth's one day and I feel a sort of final horror as I watch a boy buy a psycho-killer toy so that he can pretend he's an unstoppable maniacal murderer. What is so horrible is that this boy is doing this instinctively, for his very survival. In order to live, in order not to go mad, this boy is **acclimating** himself to the idea of the killer-maniac, because killer- maniac energy is so present in his world. He's trying to inoculate himself through play, as all children have, everywhere, in every era. He thus lets a little bit of the energy into him--that's how **inoculations** work. Too little, and he is too afraid of the world--it's too terrifying to feel powerless amid the maniacal that taken for granted around him; to feel any power at all he needs a bit of it inside him. But if he takes in too much, he could be swamped.

How horrible that he is forced to such a choice. You'd think it would be enough to stop the world in its tracks. And what can we do for him? Struggle for a different world, yes, but that won't change what's already happened to him. What can we do for that boy except be on his side, stand by his choice, and pray for the play of his struggling soul?

"On Kids and Slasher Movies" from *Letters at 3 a. m. - Reports on Endarkenment* by Michael Ventura. Copyright 1993 by Spring Data Publications, Dallas. Reprinted by permission

MODULE #4

Objectives:

1. Students will read an article on a controversial issue and be able to describe the controlling idea.
2. Students will write a brief summary of the article and be able to identify the author's reason or intent in writing the article.
3. Students will pick out at least three new vocabulary words and be able to use them in a sentence.

Assignments:

1. Read text STEP THREE.
2. Read the article, "The Failure of Feminism."
   A. Describe the controlling idea.
   B. Summarize - give at least four points that support the main idea within the article.
   C. Interpret the conflict the author is trying to establish.
3. Flashcard File - 3 words. Find three words from the text or from the article and add them to your Flashcard File.

Wisdom is oft times nearer when we stoop than when we soar.
* *William Wordsworth*

STEP THREE:

How to Attack the Controversial Issue.

In this module you are asked to answer questions about an article in which the author has written about a controversial issue. The first question that needs to be answered is: What is a controversial issue? Webster's dictionary defines controversy as **contention**, an argument or debate. So, a controversial issue is an issue that can be debated. That means there has to be at least two different points of view on the same issue. In this module, we are going to examine how to locate and determine important ways that we can critically think about an issue that might have several different perspectives or points of view.

The first thing you need to know about any controversial piece of writing is an understanding of exactly why the author wrote the article. The author chose the topic to express his or her opinion on a particular subject. So, it is **imperative** that you **comprehend** the author's meaning. What the writer is talking about is called the controlling idea. This is similar to the topic sentence in a paragraph. The controlling idea is going to be the idea or issue upon which the entire article is going to be based.

The controlling idea of an article revolves around a position the author wants to take concerning an issue. For example, an author might want to give their opinion on the controversy connected with the issue of gays in the military. The issue in this particular instance is 'should there be gays in the military,' but the author might not give the reader the chance to decide. The article may begin with a statement that was either for or against the question. This is where the critical thinker must be alerted. To make an objective and logical decision about a topic, the reader must be able to discern the author's intent.

The author provides evidence to support his or her controlling idea. To do this he or she must furnish the reader with a number of examples, statistics, endorsements or common sense judgments that support his or her point of view. The main points the author uses will be the 'meat and potatoes' of the argument. So, to summarize the article you must choose the main points that support the controlling idea. The ability to summarize is the second way a critical thinker attacks a controversial piece of literature. A strong summary will allow the reader to see the component parts of a particular article and, therefore, allow them to make a more **distinct** evaluation of the evidence. In the following exercise you will be asked to make these judgments. Consider each of the ways closely. It will bring you one step closer to being a critical thinker.

THE FAILURE OF FEMINISM

Kay Ebling

The other day I had the world's fastest blind date. A Yuppie from Ereka penciled me in for 50 minutes on a Friday and met me at a watering hole in the rural northern California town of Arcata. He breezed in, threw his jammed daily planner on the table and shot questions at me watching my reactions as if it were a job interview. He eyed how much I drank. Then he breezed out to his next appointment. He had given us 50 minutes to size each other up and see if there were any chance for romance. His exit was so fast that as we left he let the door slam back in my face. It was an interesting slam.

Most of our 50-minute conversation had covered the changing state of male-female relationships. My blind date was 40 years old, from the Experimental Generation. He is "actively pursuing new ways for men and women to interact now that old traditions no long exist." That's a real quote. He really did say that, when I asked him what he liked to do. This was a man who had read "Ms Magazine" and believed every word. He'd been single for 16 years but had lived with a few women during that time. He was off that evening for a ski weekend, meeting someone who was paying her own way for the trip.

I, too, am from the Experimental Generation, but I couldn't even pay for my own drink. To me, feminism has backfired against women. In 1973 I left what could have been a perfectly good marriage, taking with me a child in diapers, a 10-year old Plymouth and Volume 1, Number One of Ms Magazine". I was convinced I could make it on my own. In the last 15 years my ex has married or lived with a succession of women. As he gets older, his women stay in their 20's. Meanwhile, I've stayed unattached. He drives a BMW. I ride buses.

Today I see feminism as the Great Experiment That Failed, and women in my generation, its **perpetrator**s, are the casualties. Many of us, myself included, are saddled with raising children alone. The resulting poverty makes us experts at cornmeal recipes and ways to find free recreation on weekends. At the same time, single men from our generation amass fortunes in CDs and real-estate ventures so they can breeze off on ski weekends. Feminism freed men, not women. Now men are spared the nuisance of a wife and family to support. After childbirth, if his wife's waist doesn't return to 20 inches, the husband can go out and get a more petite woman, It's far more difficult for the wife, now tied down with a baby, to

Perpetrators
Those guilty of a crime

161

find a new man. My blind date that Friday waved goodbye as he drove off in his RV. I walked home and paid the sitter with laundry quarters.

The main message of feminism was: woman, you don't need a man; remember, those of you around 40, the phrase: "A woman without a man is like a fish without a bicycle?" That joke circulated through "consciousness raising" groups across the country in the 70's. It was a philosophy that made divorce and **cohabitation** casual and routine. Feminism made women disposable. So today a lot of females are around 40 and single with a couple of kids to raise on their own. Child-support payments might pay for a few pairs of shoes, but in general, feminism gave men all the financial and personal advantages over women.

Cohabitation
Living together

What's worse, we asked for it. Many women decided: you don't need a family structure to raise your children. We packed them off to day-care centers where they could get their nurturing from professionals. Then we put on our suits and ties, packed our briefcases and took off on this Great Experiment, convinced that there was no difference between ourselves and the guys in the other offices. **'Biological** thing': How wrong we were. Because like it or not, women have babies. It's the biological thing that's just there; these organs we're born with. The truth is, a woman can't live a true feminist life unless she denies her childbearing biology. She has to live on the pill, or have her tubes tied at an early age. Then she can keep up with the guys with an uninterrupted career and then, when she's 30, she'll be paying her own way on ski weekends too.

Biological thing characteristic of living organism

The reality of feminism is a lot of frenzied overworked women dropping kids off at day-care centers. If the child is sick, they just send some children's Tylenol and then rush off to underpaid jobs that they don't even like. Two of my working-mother friends told me they were mopping floors and folding laundry after midnight last week. They live on about five hours of sleep, and it shows in their faces. And they've got husbands! I'm not advocating that women **retrogress** to the brainless housewives of the 50's who spent their afternoons baking macaroni sculptures and keeping Betty Crocker files. Post- World War II women were the first to be left with a lot of free time, and they weren't too creative in filling it. Perhaps feminism was a reaction to the Brainless Betty, and in that respect, feminism has served a purpose.

Retrogress move backward

Women should get educations so they can be brainy in the way they raise their children. Women can start small businesses, do consulting, write freelance out of the home. But women don't belong in 12-hour-a-day executive office positions, and I can't figure out today what ever made us think we would want to be there in the first place. As long as that biology is there, women can't compete equally with men. A ratio cannot be made using **disproportionate** parts. Women and men are not equal, we're different. The economy might even improve if women came home, opening up jobs for unemployed men, who could then suppor a wife and children, the way it was, prefeminism.

Dispropotion-ate
unequal comparison

Sometimes on Saturday nights I'll get dressed up and go out club-hopping or the theater, but the sight of all those other women my age, dressed a little too young, made up to high encroaching wrinkles, looking hopefully into the crowds, usually depresses me. I end up coming home, to spend my Saturday night with my daughter asleep in her room nearby. At least the NBC Saturday night lineup is geared **demographically** to women at home alone.

Demographically
science of vital statistics relating to birth and death, etc.

"The Failure of Feminism" by Kay Ebling. Copyright 1990 by Newsweek, Inc. Reprinted by permission

MODULE #5

Objectives:

1. Students will read an article on a controversial issue and be able to describe the controlling idea.
2. Students will write a brief summary and be able to express four points that support the author's view.
3. Students will identify the conflict that is being raised and describe the position the author is taking on the issue.

Assignments:

1. Read the article "The Ambivalence of Abortion."
   A. Describe the controlling idea.
   B. Summarize the article by identifying four major points the author is using to support the controlling idea.
   C. Interpret the conflict (the opposing views) the author is trying to establish.
2. Flashcard File - 3 new words

A man learns to skate by staggering about making a fool of himself; in deed. he progresses in all things by making a fool of himself.
* George Bernard Shaw

THE AMBIVALENCE OF ABORTION
Linda Bird Francke

Ambivalence
uncertainty

We were sitting in a bar on Lexington Avenue when I told my husband I was pregnant. It is not a memory I like to dwell on. Instead of the champagne and hope which had heralded the **impending** births of the first, second and third child, the news of this one was greeting with shocked silence and Scotch. "Jesus," my husband kept saying to himself, stirring the ice cubes around and around, "oh, Jesus."

Impending
upcoming

Rationalize
Defend

Oh, how we tried to **rationalize** it that night as the starting time for the movie came and went. My husband talked about his plans for a career change in the next year, to stem the staleness that fourteen years with the same investment-banking firm had brought him. A new baby would **preclude** that option.

Preclude
Stop or prevent

The timing wasn't right for me either. Having juggled pregnancies and child care with what free-lance jobs I could fit in between feedings, I had just taken on a full-time job. A new baby would put me right back in the nursery just when our youngest child was finally school age. It was time for us, we tried to rationalize. There just wasn't room in our lives now for another baby. We both agreed. And agreed. And agreed.

How very considerate they are at the Women's Services, known formally as the Center for Reproductive and Sexual Health. Yes, indeed, I could have an abortion that very Saturday morning and be out in time to drive to the country that afternoon. Bring a first morning urine specimen, a sanitary belt and napkins, a money order or $125 cash - and a friend.

My friend turned out to be my husband, standing awkwardly and ill at ease as men always do in places that are exclusively for women, as I check in at nine a.m. Other men hovered around just as anxiously, knowing they had to be there, wishing they weren't. No one spoke to each other. When I would be cycled out of there four hours later, the same men would be slumped in their same seats, locked downcast in their cells of embarrassment.

Dispirited
Depressed, dejected

The Saturday morning women's group was more **dispirited** than the men in the waiting room. There were around fifteen of us, a mixture of races, ages and backgrounds. Three girls didn't speak English at all and a fourth, a pregnant Puerto Rican girl around eighteen, translated for them.

There were six black women and a hodgepodge of whites, among them a t-shirted teenager who kept leaving the room to throw up and a puzzled middle-aged woman from Queens with three grown children.

"What form of birth control were you using?" the volunteer asked each of us. The answer was **inevitably** "none." She then went on to describe the various forms of birth control available at the clinic, and offered them to each of us.

Inevitably
predictably

The youngest Puerto Rican girl was asked through the interpreter which she'd like to use: the loop, diaphragm or pill. She shook her head "no" three times. You don't want to come back here again, do you?" the volunteer pressed. The girl's head was so low her chin rested on her breastbone. "Si," she whispered.

We had been there two hours by that time, filling out endless forms, giving blood and urine, receiving lectures. But unlike any other group of women I've been in, we didn't talk. Our **common denominator**, the one which usually floods across language and economic barriers into familiarity, today was one of shame. We were losing life that day, not giving it.

Common Denominator
Shared trait

The group kept getting cut back to smaller, more workable units and finally I was put in a small waiting room with just two other women. We changed into paper bathrobes and paper slippers, and we rustled whenever we moved. One of the women in my room was shivering and an aide brought her a blanket.

"What's the matter?" the aide asked her, "I'm scared," the women said. "How much will it hurt?" The aide smiled, "Oh nothing worse than a couple of bad cramps," she said. "This afternoon you'll be dancing a jig."

I began to panic. Suddenly the **rhetoric**, the abortion marches I'd walked in, the telegrams sent to Albany to counteract the Friends of the Fetus, the Zero Population Growth buttons I'd worn, peeled away, and I was all alone with my microscopic baby. There were just the two of us there, and soon, because it was more convenient for me and my husband, there would be one again.

Rhetoric
artificial eloquence

How could it be that I, who am so **neurotic** about life that I step over bugs rather than on them, who spends hours planting flowers and vegetables in the spring even though we rent out the house and never see them, who make sure the children are vaccinated and inoculated and filled with vitamin C, could so arbitrarily decide that this life shouldn't be.

Neurotic
Erratically concerned

"It's not a life," my husband had argued, more to convince himself than me. "It's a bunch of cells smaller than my fingernail."

Taut
tight

But any women who has had children knows that certain feeling in her **taut** swollen breasts, and slight but constant ache in her uterus that signals the arrival of a life. Though I would march myself into blisters for a women's right to exercise the option of motherhood, I discovered there in the waiting room that I was not the modern women I thought I was. When my name was called, my body felt so heavy the nurse had to help me into the examining room. I waited for my husband to burst through the door and yell "stop," but of course he didn't. I concentrated on three black spots in the acoustic ceiling until they grew in size to the shape of saucers, while the doctor swabbed my insides with antiseptic.

Divert
Change
direction

"You're going to feel a burning sensation now," he said, injecting Novocain in the neck of the womb. The pain was swift and severe, and the black saucers quivered in the air. "Stop," I cried. "Please stop." He shook his head, busy with his equipment. "It's too late to stop now," he said. "It'll just take a few more seconds."

What good sports we women are. And how obedient. Physically the pain passed even before the hum of the machine signaled that the vacuuming of my uterus was completed, my baby sucked up like ashes after a cocktail party. Ten minutes to finish. And I was back on the arm of the nurse. There were twelve beds in the recovery room. Each one had a gaily flowered draw sheet and a soft green or blue thermal blanket. It was all very feminine. Lying on these beds for an hour or more were the shocked victims of their sex, their full wombs now stripped clean,

Encumbered
burdened

their futures less **encumbered**.

It was very quiet in that room. The only voice was that of the nurse, locating the new women who had just come in so she could monitor their blood pressure, and checking out the recovered women who were free to leave.

Juice was being passed about, and I found myself sipping a Dixie cup of Hawaiian Punch. An older woman with tightly curled bleached hair was just getting up from the next bed. "That was no goddamn snap," she said resting before putting on her miniskirt and high white boots. Other women came and went, some walking out as dazed as they had entered, others with a bounce that signaled they were going right back to Bloomingdale's.

Finally then, it was time for me to leave. I checked out, making an appointment to return in two weeks for an IUD insertion. My husband was slumped in the waiting room, clutching a single yellow rose wrapped in a wet paper towel and stuffed into a Baggie.

We didn't talk the whole way home, but just held hands very tightly. At home there were more yellow roses and a tray in bed for me, and the children's curiosity to divert.

It had certainly been a successful operation. I didn't bleed at all for two days just as they had predicted, and then I bled only moderately for another four days. Within a week my breasts had subsided and the tenderness vanished, and my body felt mine again instead of the eggshell it becomes when it's protecting someone else.

And it certainly does make more sense to be having a baby right now – we say that to each other all the time. But I have this ghost now. A very little ghost that only appears when I'm seeing something beautiful, like the full moon on the ocean last weekend. And the baby waves at me. And I wave at the baby. "Of course, we have room," I cry to the ghost. "Of course, we do."

MODULE #6

Objectives:

1. Students will read an article about a controversial issue and be able to describe the controlling idea of the article.
2. Students will write a brief summary and be able to express five points that support the author the author's view.
3. Students will ascertain the conflict that is being raised and pick out the position the author is taking on the issue.

Assignments:

1. Read STEP FOUR, below
2. Read the Article, "The Gap Between Gay and Straight."
   A. Describe the controlling idea.
   B. Summarize - state four main points within the article that support the controlling idea.
   C. Interpret the conflict the author is trying to establish.
   D. Flashcard File - 3 words.

STEP FOUR

In this module we are going to explore ways to decide if what you are reading or hearing is creditable. You are beginning to make decisions based on objective criteria. To grasp the intent of the author you must be able to understand his or her meaning. The author wants you to believe that his or her point of view is the correct one. This takes us to the next important way a critical thinker understands a controversial article. What is the author's view on the controversy? Is the author for or against the issue involved? If you can decide what it is the author wants you to believe, then you can begin making judgments about the credibility of their argument.

INSTRUCTIONS: Read the article, "The Gap Between Gay and Straight". Find the controlling idea in the article and identify the author's view of the conflict. Summarize the article by picking out at least five important points that the author uses to support her position.

No student knows his subject: the most he knows is where and how to find out the things he does not know.   *Woodrow Wilson*

THE GAP BETWEEN GAY AND STRAIGHT
Barbara Ehrenreich

A strange unspoken assumption about human sexuality runs through the current debate on gay rights. Both sides agree, without saying so explicitly that the human race consists of two types of people there are heterosexuals and - on the other side of the great sexual dividing line - homosexuals. Heterosexuals are thought to be the majority, while the gays and lesbians are the "minority" **analogous** to African Americans, Latinos or any other ethnic group. Thus we have Gay Pride marches, just as we have St. Patrick's Day Parades or Puerto Rican Day. Gay militants have even rallied, in some cities, around the idea of a "queer nation."

Analogous
similar

There are ways in which this **tribalistic** view of human sexuality is useful and possibly progressive. Before the gay rights movement, homosexuality was conceived as a diffuse menace attached to no particular group and potentially threatening everyone, at least in its "**latent**" form. So, naturally, as gays came out, they insisted on a unique and prideful group identify: We're queer, and we're here! How else do you get ahead in America except banding together and hoisting a flag?

Tribalistic
Group
culture

Latent
dormant

A few recent studies seem to confirm that homosexuality is as genetically based as being blue-eyed or left-handed. And heterosexuals, whether out of tolerance or spite, have been only too happy to concede to gays a special and probably congenital identity of their own. It's a way of saying, We're on this side of the great sexual divide - and you're on that.

There's only one problem with the theory of gays-as-ethnic group: it denies the true **plasticity** of human sexuality and, in doing so, helps heterosexuals evade that which they really fear. And what heterosexuals really fear is not that "they" - an alien subgroup with attention, but that they" might well be us.

Plasticity
molded

Yes, certainly there are people who have always felt themselves to be gay - or straight - since the first unruly grade-school crush or tickle in the groin. But for every study suggesting that homosexuality is innate, there are plenty of others that suggest human sexuality is far more versatile - or **capricious**, if you like. A 1989 study by researchers affiliated with the National Academy of Sciences found that 20% of American men had had sex with a man at least once. Interestingly, in other studies, men who had served in the military reported somewhat more same-sex encounters than men who had not. Either "bisexuality" is a very common condition, or another artificial category concealing the real overlaps.

Capricious
Sudden
change in
mind

In some cultures, it is more or less accepted that "straight" men will nonetheless have sex with other men. The rapid spread of AIDS in Brazil, for example, is attributed to homosexual behavior on the part of **ostensibly** heterosexual males. the British upper class, homosexual experience used to be a not uncommon featu of male adolescence. Young Robert Graves went off to World War I pining desperately for his schoolboy lover, but returned and eventually married. And, no, he did not spend his time in the trenches buggering his comrades-in-arms.

Ostensibly
outward

So being gay is not quite the same as being Irish. There are shadings; there are changes in the course of a lifetime. I know people who were once brazenly out of the closet and are now happily heterosexually married - as well as people who have gone in the opposite direction. Or, to generalize beyond genital sexuality to realm of affection and loyalty: we all know men who are militantly straight yet reserve their deepest feelings for the male-bonded group - the team, the volunteer fire department, the men they went to war with.

The problem for the military is not that discipline will be undermined by a sudden influx of stereotypical swishy gays. The problem is that the military is still a largely unisexual institution, with all that implies about the possibility of homosexual encounters even among otherwise straight men. The traditionalists keep bringing up the crowded showers" much like the dreaded unisex toilets of the ERA debate. But, somewhere deep in the sexual imagination, one has to wonder: Why do they have to have such crowded showers anyway?

By saying that gays are a definite, distinguishable minority that can easily be excluded, the military may feel better about its own presumptive heterosexuality. But can "gays" really be excluded? Do 18 year- old recruits really have a firm idea what their sexuality is? The military could deal with its sex crisis much more simply, and justly, by ceasing to be such a unisexual institution and letting women serve on an equal basis.

Perhaps we have all, "gays" and "straights," got as far as we can with the metaphor of gays as a quasi-ethnic group entitled to its own "rights." Perhaps it is time to acknowledge that the potential to fall in love with, or just be attracted to, a person of the same sex is widespread among otherwise perfectly conventional people.

There would still be an enormous struggle over what is "right" and "wrong," "normal" and "abnormal." But at least this would have a stake in: those who think themselves as gay because of who they are; those who think themselves as straight because of who they might yet become. Quite apart from sex, all men would surely be better off in a world where simple acts of affection between men occasioned no great commentary or suspicion, where a hug would be a hug and not a "statement"

MODULE #7

Objectives:

1. Students will read an article on a controversial issue and be able to give all the information asked in module #6
2. Students will pick out at least three new vocabulary words and be able to use them in a sentence.
3. Students will equate the processing of particular information from the articles to levels of thinking in Bloom's Taxonomy.

ASSIGNMENTS:

1. Read the article, "Who's Afraid of the Big Bad Bang"
   a. Identify the controlling idea within the article.
   b. Summarize the article and state the main points that support the controlling idea.
   c. Describe the conflict and discuss the author's position on the conflict.
   d. See handout on Bloom's Taxonomy in the appendix page u-v.
   e. Flashcard file - 3 words.

The test of a first rate intelligence is the ability to hold two opposing ideas at the same time, and still retain the ability to junction.

*F Scott Fitzgerald

WHO'S AFRAID OF THE BIG BAD BANG
Dennis Overbye

Scientists, it seems are becoming the new villains of Western society. Once portrayed as heroes, they now appear in movies betraying Sigourney Weaver to bring home an alien for "the company" or being oblivious to Susan Sarandon's desperate search for a cure for her son. We read about them in the newspapers faking and stealing data, and we see them in front of Congressional committees defending billion-dollar research budgets. We hear them in sound bites trampling our sensibilities by comparing the Big Bang or some subatomic particle to God.

Polemic
Argument about doctrines

Last summer a journalist named Bryan Appleyard rode the discontent to the top of England's best-seller lists with a neoconservative **polemic** called *Understanding the Present, subtitled Science and the Soul of Modern Man*. In Britain, the book inspired headlines such as FOR GOD'S SAKE FIRE THE BIG BANG BRIGADE. Its publication in the US has begun to strike sparks. Science, maintains Appleyard, devalues questions it can't answer, such as the meaning of life or the existence of God. Its relentless advance has driven the magic out of the world, leaving us with nothing to believe in. With no standards, liberal

Relativism
Close in connection

democracies descend into moral anarchy and cultural **relativism**. Once Galileo looked through that telescope, it seems, the Los Angeles riots were only a matter of time. Science, he concluded ominously, must be "humbled."

Appleyard would lay the woes of the 20th Century at Stephen Hawking's wheelchair. Commenting on Hawking's oft expressed hope that physicists may soon construct a theory that would unite all the forces of nature into one mathematical equation suitable for a T-shirt, a so-called theory of everything, he declaims alarmingly that it could be used to predict that a "particular snowflake would fall on a particular blade of grass or that you would be reading this now." Never mind that such determinist ambitions died long ago with the discovery of quantum uncertainty. Faced with that prospect, who would not reach for the candles and tarot cards?

Acquiesced
agreed

Scientists are partly to blame for this mess. They have silently **acquiesced** in the proposition that if we just keep writing checks and leaving them alone, science could solve the problems of the world. They have promoted the presentation of themselves as antiseptic drones, whose work is uncorrupted by influences like sex, greed or ambition, which muddy life for the rest of us. But science is done by real people who do not check their humanity at the lab door.

Lamentably but humanly, they do shoot their mouths off too much about God and the **egregiously** misnamed theory of everything. The Young Turks of every generation for the past hundred years have proclaimed the imminent end of physics, but every advance has only opened new vistas of mysteries. There is no reason to think we know the right questions yet, let alone ultimate answers. The currency of science is not truth, but doubt.

And, **paradoxically**, faith. Science is nothing if not a spiritual undertaking. The idea that nature forms some sort of coherent whole, a universe, ruled by laws accessible to us, is a faith. The creation and end of the universe are theological notions, not astronomical ones.

We can only wonder whether some law or laws will stand revealed some day at the end of the grudging trial-and-error process of science. The theory of everything, even if it existed, however, could not pretend to tell us what we most want to know. It could not tell us why the universe exists - why there is something rather than nothing at all. And it could not tell us if our lives have meaning, if God loves us.

Written on a piece of paper or on a T-shirt, the theory of everything would just lie there waiting for something else to breathe fire into it. The question of whether the universe is a steady state or a Big Bang, or whether it has 10 dimensions or four, is just decorative trim around the grand mystery of why anything or any law exists. But by reminding us of our deep cosmic ignorance, science, far from dulling the mystery of existence, sharpens it the way garlic wafting on the evening breeze whets your appetite. It reminds us that we dwell in a mystery that is ultimately more to be savored than solved.

On God's love science is also silent, and that silence is the wind of liberation. Physicists can neither prove nor disapprove that Jesus turned water into wine, only that such a transformation is improbable under the present admittedly provisional physical laws. Quantum theory and tensor equations are part of nature as trees and rains and sex. We are, all of us, including Appleyard, free to make what we want of it. We are free to wake up every morning grateful for the feeling of sunshine on our face or grumpy for the prospect of tomorrow's rain. The fact that science cannot find any purpose to the universe does not mean there is not one. We are free to construct parables for our moral **edification** out of the law of the jungle, or out of the evolution and interdependence of the species. But the parables we choose will only reflect the values we have already decided to enshrine.

If this be alienation, make the most of it. We could have used a little more in, say, Nazi Germany. If history teaches us anything, it is to beware people who know the truth. Appleyard and his neoconservative friends moan about the demise of moral and cultural authority and bash liberal democracy because it fails to choose. But the failure to choose is itself a choice. What it chooses is that people are, or can be, grown-ups. That too is a value, the notion that we all individually or collectively may Be the salvation of one another. Cosmic ignorance does not diminish us, it ennobles us.

MODULE #8

Objectives:

1. Students will be able to read a controversial article and fulfill the requirements of module #7. They will also be able to describe how the author employs persuasive techniques to convince the reader that his/hers is the correct side of the issue.
   Techniques Used to Persuade:
   A. Statistics
   B. Logic/Common Sense
   C. Case studies
   D. Expert testimony
   F. Endorsement
   F. Humor/Sarcasm

2. Students will be able to pick out at least three new vocabulary words and use them in a sentence.

Assignments:

1. Read text STEP FIVE.
2. Read the article, "On Becoming A Chicano"
   a. State the Controlling idea of the article.
   b. Summarize the article using at least five points that support the controlling point.
   c. Identify the conflict in the article.
   d. Discuss the author's view of the conflict.
   e. Describe the techniques the author uses to illustrate his/her point of view.

When I was 14, my father was so ignorant I could hardly stand to have the old man around But when I was 21, I was astonished at how much the old man had learned in seven years.
* Mark Twain

STEP FIVE: How to Persuade

In this module we are going to look at six techniques an author might use to try to **persuade** the reader that their point of view is the right one. As listed in the objectives of this Module, the following are some of the basic ways an author uses to influence the reader:

1. Statistics
2. Logic/Common sense
3. Case studies
4. Expert testimony
5. Endorsement
6. Humor/sarcasm

The first method is to use statistics to back up their position. For example, a writer might say that 23% of all deaths in America are related to drinking alcohol. Obviously, the author in this case is trying to make an argument against drinking alcohol. The critical reader is going to have a number of questions that will test the credibility of this statistic.

First, the critical thinker knows that not all statistics are accurate. So, the first question the reader might ask is: What is the source of this statistic? Is the source reliable? Is the information available in its original form? Each one of these questions is going to help the reader begin to make judgments about the credibility of the statistic and whether or not they should be persuaded by it.

Assumption
Takes for
granted

The second way an author might use to try to influence the reader is by using logic or common sense. In this method, the author makes an **assumption** that is not necessarily substantiated. For example, the author may say in an article that is trying to persuade you about voting for a school budget, that "everyone wants to have better schools." The author is making an assumption based not on any statistical evidence, but on a belief that many or most of all people who are reading the article are going to agree with the position without being given any additional information. The critical thinker is always **skeptical** about unsupported information.

Skeptical
doubtful

Case studies are a third method used by writers when they are trying to convince the reader about a position. A case study is simply giving an example of a particular point or view. The case study is used to portray what the author is trying to prove. To illustrate this, an author might write in an article that is against abortion, a **scenario** about a child who was **potentially** going to be aborted (by a young unwed mother or poor couple who already have children) and is now a grown happy child. The author is showing the reader that this type of circumstance can happen and tries to convince them it is a mistake. The critical thinker is quick not to make generalizations based on a single case. The critical thinker would try to search out other scenarios that would give a more balanced view of a particular issue.

Scenario
Outline of a drama

Potentially
possibly

The fourth technique used by an author when trying to convince a reader is by using expert **testimony**. In this case the author is going to try to influence the reader by bringing up evidence given by **alleged** experts in a field. For example, if a writer wanted to convince you about some medical issue, they might have a doctor who supported the author's view give testimony about the issue. Or if it were a legal issue, they would use a lawyer's opinion. Again, the critical thinker seeks out other's points of view. He or she knows that not all lawyers agree on every issue or that doctors have differences of opinion.

Testimony
Statement under oath

Alleged
supposed

A fifth way a writer tries to convince is by having a **prominent** or popular person or group support their position. If former President Regan, came out in support of a new medical procedure or a rock star stated he was in favor of a legislative policy, it does not mean that they understand the issues involved or that they have any particular knowledge that would make their judgments any better than your own. Therefore, the critical thinker is not influenced by name alone. The critical thinker searches for creditable evidence that can be supported objectively.

Prominent
leading

The sixth and last technique (at least for the purposes of this manual) an author **utilizes** to try to persuade the reader is by using humor or sarcasm to convince. Many times humor or sarcasm is used in a negative way. It is negative in the sense that the author is not trying to convince the reader to believe in an issue, but is trying to persuade them that a particular issue or point of view is silly, unreasonable, or illogical. For example, if a writer wanted to discredit another person's view they may make fun of or **exaggerate** a particular flaw that person exhibits. Former President, Gerald Ford had a number of on-TV camera incidents where he tripped or fell down. On a number of occasions political columnists would bring up these mishaps, even when they didn't apply to the issue; i.e., "On another one of the President's trips."

Utilizes
uses

Exaggerate
Beyond the truth

Humor and sarcasm can be a powerful tool, but it must be handled wisely and with **discretion**. The critical thinker stays objective and stays away from the cheap shot.

Discretion
Freedom to make choices

ON BECOMING A CHICANO
Richard Rodriguez

Today, I am only technically the person I once felt myself to be: a Mexican American, a Chicano. Partly because I had no way of comprehending my racial identity except in this technical sense, I gave up long ago the cultural consequences of being a Chicano.

Assumption
Takes for
granted

Entail
involve

The change came gradually but early. When I was beginning grade school, I noted to myself the fact that the classroom environment was so different in its styles and **assumptions** from my own family environment that survival would essentially **entail** a choice between both worlds. When I became a student, I was literally "remade"; neither I nor my teachers considered anything I had known before as relevant. I had to forget most of what my culture had provided, because to remember it was a disadvantage. The past and its cultural values became detachable, like a piece of clothing grown heavy on a warm day and finally put away.

Strangely, the discovery that I have been inattentive to my cultural past has arisen because others--student colleagues and faculty members--have started to assume that I am a Chicano. The ease with which the assumption is made forces me to suspect that the label is not meant to suggest cultural, but racial, identity. Nonetheless, as a graduate student and a prospective university faculty member; I am routinely expected to assume intellectual leadership as a member of a racial minority. Recently, for example, I heard the moderator of a panel discussion introduce me as "Richard Rodriguez, a Chicano intellectual." I wanted to correct the speaker--because I felt guilty representing a non-academic cultural tradition that I had willingly abandoned. So I can only guess what it would have meant to have retained my culture as I entered the classroom, what it would mean for me to

Juxtaposed
Placed side
by side for
comparison

be today a "Chicano intellectual." (The two words **juxtaposed** excite me; for years I thought a Chicano had to decide between being one or the other.)

Does the fact that I barely spoke any English until I was nine, or that as a child I felt a surge of self-hatred whenever a passing teenager would yell a racial slur, or that I saw my skin darken each summer--do any of these facts shape the ideas which I have or am capable of having? Today, I suspect they do--in ways I doubt the moderator who referred to me as a "Chicano intellectual" intended. The peculiar status of being a "Chicano intellectual" makes me grow restless at the thought that I have lost at least as much as I have gained through education.

I remember when, 20 years ago, two grammar-school nuns visited my childhood home. They had come to suggest--with more tact than was necessary, because my parents accepted without question the church's authority--that we make a greater effort to speak as much English around the house as possible. The nuns realized that my brothers and I led solitary lives largely because we were barely able to comprehend English in a school where we were the only Spanish-speaking students. My mother and father complied as best they could. Heroically, they gave up speaking to us in Spanish--the language that formed so much of the family's sense of intimacy in an alien world--and began to speak a broken English. Instead of Spanish sounds, I began hearing sounds that were new, harder; less friendly. More important, I was encouraged to respond in English.

The change in language was the most dramatic and obvious indication that I would become very much like the "gringo "--a term which was used descriptively rather than **pejoratively** in my home--and unlike the Spanish- speaking relatives who largely constituted my preschool world. Gradually, Spanish became a sound freighted with only a kind of sentimental significance, like the sound of the bedroom clock I listened to in my aunt's house when I spent the night. Just as gradually, English became the language I came not to hear because it was the language I used every day, as I gained access to a new, larger society. But the memory of Spanish persisted as a reminder of the society I had left. I can remember occasions when I entered a room and my parents were speaking to one another in Spanish; seeing me, they shifted into their more formalized English. Hearing them speak to me in English troubled me. The bond their voices once secured was loosened by the new tongue.

Pejoratively
negatively

This is not to suggest that I was being forced to give up my Chicano past. After the initial awkwardness of transition, I committed myself, fully and freely, to the culture of the classroom. Soon what I was learning in school was so **antithetical** to what my parents knew and did that I was careful about the way I talked about myself at the evening dinner table. Occasionally, there were moments of childish cruelty: a son's condescending to instruct either one of his parents about a "simple" point of English pronunciation or grammar.

Antithetical
contradictory

Social scientists often remark, about situations such as mine, that children feel a sense of loss as they move away from their working class identifications and models. Certainly, what I experienced, others have also whatever their race. Like other generations, of say, Polish-American or Irish- American children coming home from college, I was to know the silence that ensues so quickly after the quick exchange of news and the dwindling of common interests.

In addition, however; education seemed to mean not only a gradual dissolving of familial and class ties but also a change of racial identity. The new language I spoke was only the most obvious reason for my associating the classroom with "gringo" society. The society I knew as Chicano was barely literate--in English or Spanish--and so impatient with either prolonged reflection or abstraction that I found the academic environment a sharp contrast. Sharpening the contrast was the stereotype of the Mexican as a mental inferior. (The fear of this stereotype has been so deep that only recently have I been willing to listen to those, like D. H. Lawrence, who celebrate the "non-cerebral" Mexican as an alternative to the rational and scientific European man.) Because I did not know how to distinguish the healthy non-rationality of Chicano culture from the mental incompetence of which Chicanos were unjustly accused, I was willing to abandon my non- mental skills in order to disprove the racist's stereotype.

Repudiate
reject

I was wise enough not to feel proud of the person education had helped me to become. I knew that education had led me to **repudiate** my race. I was frequently labeled a *pocho*. a Mexican with gringo pretensions, not only because I could not speak Spanish but also because I would respond in English with precise and careful sentences. Uncles would laugh good- naturedly, but I detected scorn in their voices. For my grandmother, the least **assimilated** of my relations, the changes in her grandson since entering school were especially troubling. She remains today a dark and silently critical figure in my memory, a reminder of the Mexican-Indian ancestry that somehow my educational success has violated.

Assimilated
Absorbed
merged

Nonetheless, I became more comfortable reading or writing careful prose than talking to a kitchen filled with listeners, withdrawing from situations to reflect on their significance rather than grasping for meaning at the scene. I remember, one August evening, slipping away from a gathering of aunts and uncles in the backyard, going into a bedroom tenderly lighted by a late sun, and opening a novel about life in nineteenth century England. There, by an open window, reading, I was barely conscious of the sounds of laughter outside.

Barrio-
Section of a
city inhabited
by Spanish
speaking
people

With so few fellow Chicanos in the university, I had no chance to develop an alternative consciousness. When I spent occasional weekends tutoring lower class Chicano teenagers or when I talked with Mexican-American janitors and maids around the campus, there was a kind of sympathy-a sense, however privately held-that we knew something about one another. But I regarded them all primarily as people from my past. The maids reminded me of my aunts (similarly employed); the students I tutored reminded me of my cousins (who also spoke English with **barrio** accents).

When I was young, I was taught to refer to my ancestry as Mexican American. Chicano was a word used among friends or relatives. It implied a familiarity based on shared experience. Spoken casually, the term easily became an insult. In 1968 the word Chicano was about to become a political term. I heard it shouted into microphones as Third World groups agitated for increased student and faculty representation in higher education. It was not long before I became a Chicano in the eyes of students and faculty members. My racial identity was assumed for only the simplest reasons: my skin color and last name.

On occasion I was asked to account for my interests in Renaissance English literature. When I explained them, declaring a need for cultural assimilation, on the campus, my listener would disagree. I sensed suspicion on the part of a number of my fellow minority students. When I could not imitate Spanish pronunciations or the dialect of the barrio, when I was plainly uninterested in wearing ethnic costumes and could not master a special handshake that minority students often used with one another, they knew I was different. And I was. I was assimilated into the culture of a graduate department of English. As a result, I watched how in less than five years nearly every minority graduate student I knew dropped out of school, largely for cultural reasons. Often they didn't understand the value of analyzing literature in professional jargon, which others around them readily adopted. Nor did they move as readily to lofty heights of abstraction. They became easily depressed by the seeming uselessness of the talk they heard around them. "It's not for real," I still hear a minority student murmur to herself and perhaps to me, shaking her head slowly, as we sat together in a class listening to a discussion on punctuation in a Renaissance epic.

I survived--thanks to the accommodation I had made long before. In fact, I prospered, partly as a result of the political movement designed to increase the enrollment of minority students less assimilated than I in higher education. Suddenly grants, fellowships, and teaching offers became abundant.

In 1972 I went to England on a Fuibright scholarship. I hoped the months of brooding about racial identity were behind me. I wanted to concentrate on my dissertation, which the distractions of an American campus had not permitted. But the freedom I anticipated did not last for long. Barely a month after I had begun working regularly in the reading room of the British Museum, I was surprised, and even frightened, to have to acknowledge that I was not at ease living the **rarefied** life of the academic. With my pile of research file cards growing taller, the mass of secondary materials and opinions was making it harder for me to say anything original about my subject. Every sentence I wrote, every thought I had, became so

Rarefied
Lofty, elevated in style

loaded with qualifications and footnotes that it said very little. My scholarship became little more than an exercise in caution. I had an accompanying suspicion that whatever I did manage to write and call my dissertation would be of little use. Opening books so dusty that they must not have been used in decades, I began to doubt the value of writing what only a few people would read. Obviously, I was going through the fairly typical crisis of the American graduate student. But with one difference: After four years of involvement with questions of racial identity, I now saw my problems as a scholar in the context of the cultural issues that had been raised by my racial situation. So much of what my work in the British Museum lacked, my parents' culture possessed. They were people not afraid to generalize or to find insights in their generalities. More important, they had the capacity to make passionate statements, something I was beginning to doubt my dissertation would ever allow me to do. I needed to learn how to trust the use of "I" in my writing the way they trusted its use in their speech. Thus developed a persistent yearning for the very Chicano culture that I had abandoned as useless.

Feelings of depression came occasionally but forcefully. Some days I found my work so oppressive that I had to leave the reading room and stroll through the museum. One afternoon, appropriately enough, I found myself in an upstairs gallery containing Mayan and Aztec sculptures. Even there the sudden yearning for a Chicano past seemed available to me only as nostalgia. One morning, as I was reading a book about Puritan autobiography, I overheard two Spaniards whispering to one another. I did not hear what they said, but I did hear the sound of their Spanish--and it embraced me, filling my mind with swirling images of a past long abandoned.

I returned from England, disheartened, a few months later. My dissertation was coming along well, but 1 did not know whether I wanted to submit it. Worse, I did not know whether I wanted a career in higher education. I detested the prospect of spending the rest of my life in libraries and classrooms, in touch with my past only through the binoculars nostalgia makes available. I knew that I could not simply recreate a version of what I would have been like had I not become an academic. There was no possibility of going back. But if the culture of my birth was to survive, it would have to animate my academic work. That was the lesson of the British Museum.

I frankly do not know how my academic autobiography will end. Sometimes I think I will have to leave the campus, in order to reconcile my past and present. Other times, more optimistically, I think that a kind of negative reconciliation is already in progress, that I can make creative use of my sense of loss. For instance, with my sense of the cleavage between past and present, I can, as a literary critic, identify issues in Renaissance **pastoral**-a literature which records the feelings of the courtly when confronted by the alternatives of rural and rustic life. And perhaps I can speak with unusual feeling about the price we must pay, or have paid, as a rational society for confessing seventeenth-century **Cartesian** faiths. Likewise, because of my sense of cultural loss, I may be able to identify more readily than another the ways in which language has meaning simply as sound and what the printed word can and cannot give us. At the very least, I can point up the academy's tendency to ignore the cultures beyond its own horizons.

Pastoral
Artistic work evoking rural life

Cartesian
Rational, refers to French philosopher Rene Descartes (1580-1650)

On my job interview, the department chairman has been listening to an oral version of what I have just written. I tell him he should be very clear about the fact that I am not, at the moment, confident enough to call myself a Chicano. Perhaps I never will be. But as I say all this, I look at the interviewer. He smiles softly. Has he heard what I have been trying to say? I wonder. I repeat: I have lost the ability to bring my past into my present; I do not know how to be a Chicano reader of Spenser or Shakespeare. All that remains is a desire for the past. He sighs, preoccupied, looking at my records. Would I be interested in teaching a course on the Mexican novel in translation? Do I understand that part of my duties would require that I become a counselor of minority students? What was the subject of that dissertation I did in England?

Have I read the book on the same subject that was just published this month? Behind the questioner a figure forms in my imagination: my grandmother, her face solemn and still.

MODULE #9

Objectives:

1. Students will be able to read a controversial article and fulfill the requirements of Module #8.
2. Plus, they will be able to give a personal opinion on the article either agreeing with or disagreeing with the author.
3. Students will be able to support their opinion by using techniques "Authors Use to Persuade" or by citing a creditable source which would substantiate their view.
4. Students will be able to pick out at least three new vocabulary words and use them in sentences.

Assignments:

1. Read STEP SIX, "Forming Your Own Opinion."
2. Read "A Political Correction."
   A. Summarize the article and state the controlling idea and the conflict involved.
   B. Discuss the author's point of view concerning the conflict and describe the component parts of the author's argument.
   C. Give your opinion on the conflict in the article and support your opinion by evidence.
   D. Read a classmate's review of "A Political Correction," verbally pointing out omissions in the analysis or faulty reasoning used by the reviewer.
   E. Flashcard File - 3 words.

Instructions: Read the article, "A Political Correction." Find the controlling idea in the article and identify the author's view of the conflict. Give your opinion on the issue. Summarize the article by picking out at least five important points that the author uses to support his or her position. Describe the techniques the Author uses to support his or her point of view.

The wisest mind has something yet to learn.   ** George Santayana*

STEP SIX: Forming Your Own Opinion

This passage may seem silly to you. How can someone teach you to make up your own mind? Isn't that what you're already doing? But, the point of critical thinking is not to pass this course or help you pass any other course. Critical thinking is for every day. Most of us are taught to listen to our teachers, listen to our parents, listen to the government. But then we're sent out to be the parents and teachers, the policemen and presidents. What basis do we have? A hope that everything we were told was right? That's not enough. Now we know that people don't always tell the whole truth. They might want us to take their point of view, but that may not be in our best interest.

We use critical thinking to help us make decisions ranging from which car to buy to which president to elect. Making up your mind means looking at all the views of a subject carefully, seeing the strong points and weak points of an issue or situation, and ignoring the persuasive techniques. We do not want to buy a car because our friend looks good in his. We don't know how often he goes to the shop or how his gas mileage is or any number of things that makes a car good.

Procedure
action
Once you are fully informed you can start to think about the decision making process. Forming an opinion on a topic is not an emotional **procedure**. It is an intellectual one. You must weigh and consider how each side affects you and those around you. The smartest side is the one you can support well. Anyone can say "I believe this. ." But, a critical thinker should be able to say, "I understand your point of view, but I believe this because it is supported by A, B and C." Forming an opinion is not easy, but once a decision is made one can know he or she made the most informed conclusion. No one can do better than that!

Assess
examine
In this Module you are going to **assess** an author's point of view. You may not have all the information you need to state whether you think the writer is right or wrong. However, you should be able to see flaws or weaknesses in their logic, in their use of unsubstantiated assumptions or in the strength of the sources they use for their statistics.

A POLITICAL CORRECTION
Anna Quindlen

Discussions of political correctness on campus always puzzle me a bit, because they usually have as their starting point a view of the academy, in fact the world, that is contrary to established reality. That is that into this pool of calm **egalitarian** rational **discourse** comes the bigfoot of racial and gender politics, ready to stomp down anyone who offends, diverges, challenges liberal **orthodoxy**.

Egalitarian
Equal rights for all

Discourse
Conversation

Orthodoxy
approved

The stomping part I understand. But the calm egalitarian pool? Oh phooey, boys and girls.

During the final week of school, graduating college seniors could get a quick current events education about how the world works:

-A sailor was sentenced to life in prison for punching and kicking one of his fellows to death in a bathroom. The dead man was gay and had requested a discharge because of frequent harassment; his assailant admitted that he had lied to investigators when he said the beating had been prompted by the gay sailor's sexual advances.

-A Louisiana man was acquitted of shooting and killing an unarmed 16 year old Japanese exchange student who came to the wrong house looking for a Halloween party.

-Twenty-one Secret Service agents in Annapolis preparing for a visit by the President stopped at a Denny's restaurant. All but six were served in short order. The six were black. The restaurant chain faces a lawsuit in California based on similar complaints from 32 black customers.

-And finally, Senator Jesse Helms said he would not support Roberta Achtenburg for Assistant Secretary of Housing and Urban Development because she was a "damn lesbian."

Ideas should be freely exchanged not only because one woman's obscenity is another's Bovary, but because you can learn a lot of good stuff from bad stuff. At Penn, a group of black students seized and destroyed thousands of copies of the campus paper because they found offensive the writings of a conservative columnist.

During the course of their Ivy education, someone should have taught those students that a pointed exchange of letters, columns and counter columns always does more to further human understanding - and usually the just cause- than censorship. Look at Senator Helm's comments. They do not reflect badly on Ms. Achtenburg, who was confirmed, as she deserved to be. They prove that the Senator speaks his mind, and that he is not working with much when he does. Ignorant free speech often works against the speaker. That is one of the several reasons why it must be given rein instead of **suppressed**.

Suppressed
Held down,
prevented

There are complaints that because of incidents like the one at Penn, Students feel inhibited about airing their opinions on campuses that have become oversensitive to minority groups. But let's remember that for every highly publicized incident of overreaction or suppression, there is plenty of small-scale incivility and bigotry. Let's remember that there are good inhibitions, and there are bad **inhibitions**. If people can no longer discuss their differences, that is bad. If people make fewer racist jokes, that is just fine.

Inhibitions
restraints

The class of '93 has gone out to meet the world. And no matter how loud the cry about political correctness, this is the fact behind the fracas: After four short years these students enter a world in which intolerance for people - for waiting to be served breakfast or for people being beaten to death in a bathroom. Liberal orthodoxy? Phooey, boys and girls. Most of what you learn in life is something altogether different.

"A Political Correction" by Anna Quindlen Copyright 1993 by the New York Times. Reprinted by permission.

MODULE #10

Objectives:

1. Students will be able to read a controversial article and fulfill the requirements of all previous Modules. In addition, they will be able to read and orally critique the work of another student, highlighting the strengths of the work and pointing out the weakness or omissions as Established in the criteria of all previous modules.
2. Students will be able to pick out at least three vocabulary words and be able to use them in a sentence.

Assignments:

1. Read the article "Districting by Pigmentation."
   A. Summarize the article and state the controlling idea and the conflict involved.
   B. Discuss the author's point of view concerning the conflict and describe the component parts of the author's argument.
   C. Give your opinion on the conflict in the article and support your opinion by providing other evidence and parallel cases.
   D. Read a classmate's review of "Districting by Pigmentation" pointing out omissions in the analysis or faulty reasoning used by the reviewer.
   E. Flashcard File - 3 words.

He who does not understand your silence, will probably not understand your words.

*Elbert Hubbard

DISTRICTING BY PIGMENTATION
George F. Will

North Carolina's 12th Congressional District straggles down Interstate 85 and for the most part of its length is no wider than the highway. Says a state legislator, "If you drive down the interstate with both car doors open, you'd kill most of the people in the district."

The district was drawn to sweep together enough blacks to guarantee a black member of Congress if all the blacks (a slender 53 percent majority) do as the government obviously thinks they should - vote as a herd. The state drew the district under duress from Bush's Justice Department, which thought it was applying the Voting Rights Act. It is read to require the creation of many "majority minority" districts, the boundaries of which veer hither and yon, gathering in blacks or Hispanics. (Bellow is Illinois's "earmuff"district designed to corral Hispanics.)

Twenty percent of North Carolina voters are black. When redistricting after the 1990 census, North Carolina created one "safe" black district. Not enough, said Washington; hence, the 12th District.

Gerrymande ring
changes in boundaries in election districts to give unfair advantage

Now the Supreme Court has ruled 5-4 that the 12th District may amount to unconstitutional racial **gerrymandering**. Why? Perhaps whites are denied the "equal protection" right to "race neutral" electoral processes. The Court has never affirmed any such right, and hardly can without finding the VRA unconstitutional. Justice O'Conner's opinion (joined by Rehnquist, Scalia, Kennedy and Thomas) contains political maxims more convincing than its constitutional reasoning. It is

Aesthetic
Pertains to beauty

less an argument than an **aesthetic** recoil from a political act ; District 12. O'Conner's opinion sows confusion about what is permitted, or required, by the VRA in the way of racial gerrymandering.

Egregious
outrageous

"It is unsettling," says O'Conner, "how closely the North Carolina plan resembles the most **egregious** racial gerrymanders of the past." Such as Mississippi's shoestring district during the Reconstruction, which swept enough blacks into one narrow district along the river to leave five other districts with white majorities. Or such as Alabama's redrawing of the city borders of Tuskegee in the 1950's to turn a square city into a 28-side entity excluding many black voters from the city. However, O'Conner feeling "unsettled" does not constitute a constitutional argument. What should unsettle her, and us, is the many "race conscious" government actions that have brought us to monstrosities like North Carolina's 12th.

O'Conner says the bizarre shape of the 12th is "unexplainable on grounds other than race" and "reapportionment is one area in which appearances do matter." Actually, the 12 District appears compatible with the VRA, as currently construed (or misconstrued), and not incompatible with any constitutional principal of government action that the five justices affirm. They do not affirm the principle that government actions must be colorblind.

Courts have construed the VRA to mean that for blacks and Hispanics the right to a certain level of desired results: The Act effectively entitles blacks and Hispanics to a certain percentage of congressional seats.

O'Conner cites former Justice Brennan's warning that "even in the pursuit of remedial objectives, an explicit policy of assignment by race may serve to stimulate our society's latent race consciousness, suggesting the utility and propriety of basing decisions on a factor that ideally bears no relationship to an individual's worth or needs." But for two decades the government, responding to civil rights industry's lobbying for a radical spoils system (always called 'remedial"), has made race consciousness not latent but conspicuous in policy making. And the VRA obviously assumes the "utility and propriety" of basing voting decisions on skin pigmentation.

Categorical Representation. O'Connor says that a congressional district that is obviously created solely to **effectuate** the perceived common interest of one racial group "reinforces the perception that members of the same racial group regardless of their age, education, economic status, or the community in which they live - think alike, share the same political interests, and will prefer the same candidates at the polls." But the VRA promotes that "perception" as a **normative** rule. The five justices do not say that an act promoting that perception is unconstitutional. They say that when redistricting is obviously driven by racial calculations, there must be the "compelling" justification of remedying past discrimination.

Effectuate
cause

Normative
standardize

The Act implicitly affirms the doctrine of "categorical representation," which holds that the interests of a particular racial, ethnic or sexual group can only be understood, sympathized with, articulated and advanced by members of those groups. This doctrine threatens the core tenet of the nation's public philosophy - the principal that rights inhere in individuals, not groups. The leads to this

Balkanizing proposition; group thinking is natural and admirable. The Court majority offers the muddy suggestion that racial gerrymandering will pass muster if the resulting districts are not too aggressively indifferent to "compactness, **contiguousness**, geographical boundaries, or political subdivisions." Those are nice attributes of districts but are neither mandated by the Constitution nor respected by the VRA. American politics and the law will continue to be disfigured by stains like the 12th District as long as we pursue the **chimeric** justice that is produced by "race-conscious remedies" for race-conscious injustices in the past.

Contiguous-ness
Touching of borders

Chimeric
Unreal, impossible

The five justices' sensible political philosophy makes them squeamish about the VRA's promotion of particular race results. But until the justices are prepared to find the VRA, as currently construed, they, and we, will be troubled.

MODULE #11

Objectives:

1. Students will be able to read a controversial article and fulfill the requirements of all previous Modules.
2. Students will be able to read and orally critique the work of another student, highlighting the strengths of the work and pointing out the weakness or omissions as established in the criteria of all previous Modules.
3. In addition, students will be able to use parallel cases to support their opinions on the controversy.
4. Students will be able to pick out at least three vocabulary words and be able to use them in a sentence.

Assignments:

1. Read text STEP SEVEN, "Parallel Positions."
2. Read "The Melting Pot is Still Simmering."
   A. Summarize the article and state the controlling idea and the conflict involved.
   B. Discuss the author's point of view concerning the conflict and describe the author's argument.
   C. Give your opinion on the conflict in the article and support your opinion by providing other evidence and parallel cases.
   D. Read a classmate's review of "The Melting Pot is Still Simmering" pointing out omissions in the analysis or faulty reasoning used by the reviewer.
   E. Flashcard File - 3 words.

It is necessary to the happiness of a man that he be mentally faithful to himself.
* Thomas Paine

STEP SEVEN: **Parallel Positions**

In Module nine you were asked to add a new dimension to your analysis. You were asked to provide a parallel view or case study to your review. Simply stated, giving a parallel case means that you must find another situation or incident that is similar in content or intent to one you are comparing it to. This can be a
Implicit
necessary difficult task, because **implicit** in finding another situation that is similar to your issue, is the need to fully understand the matter at hand. You must be able to determine the controlling idea of the article. You need to be able to distinguish the conflict that is being argued; it is necessary that you be able to recognize the author's intent. When you have found these points, then you can search for a parallel situation where all the elements of the issue are similar. An example of a parallel situation might be, the historical parallels between Nazi Germany and Bosnia (the Muslim section of the former Yugoslavia) where people are killing
Evident
clear each other for the purpose of ethic cleansing. The similarities are **evident**. There appears to be no reason for the bloodshed, other than economic gain and the long term prejudice between various peoples. The critical thinker evaluates the common motive to see the parallel. They see the cause and effect. They look for the underlying reason. They are not satisfied with appearances. If history repeats itself, what is the cause? What needs to be changed?

Instructions: Read the article, "The Melting Pot is Still Simmering." Find the controlling idea in the article and identify the author's view of the conflict. Give your opinion on the issue and give a parallel situation from history or the present. Summarize the article by picking out at least five important points that the author uses to support his or her position. Describe the techniques the author uses to support his or her point of view.

THE MELTING POT IS STILL SIMMERING
Richard Brookhiser

America thinks of itself as a diverse society- a "gorgeous **mosaic**," in the words of New York City Mayor Dinkins; a quilt of many ethnic and racial patches, in a favorite metaphor of the Rev. Jesse Jackson's. But the figures of the 1990 census, only now crunched, suggest that the demographic surface of life in the US is a lot smoother than one thinks. So is the cultural surface, unless the politicians ruffle it.

Mosaic
Picture made of small pieces

Fifty-eight million Americans, out of a total population of 248 million, claim German ancestry. In the second place are 38 million who say they are wholly or partly Irish. Those of English ancestry come in third, at 32 million, followed by African Americans, at 23 million.

This lineup of American's major minorities has been extraordinarily stable over the years considering the top four ancestry groups of the 1980 census but also the top four of the 1 790 census, as far as one can tell from the surnames collected by the founding headcounters. The relative sizes of the big four were different then: English Americans made up almost half the population, while African Americans were one-fifth. But American has been turning up the same ethnic cards for a long time.

The stability is shown by the people Americans have put into the White House. Every US President except for the all-Dutch Martin Van Buren has descended whole or part from the three largest white demographic groups. In the 1980's the Democrats tried to vary the mix by fielding Norwegian-Italian and Greek-Danish tickets. Last year they reverted to form and managed to replace George Herbert Walker Bush with William Jefferson Clinton.

This is a pretty simple mosaic, at least as far as its biggest pieces are concerned, and the consequences for cultural integration and social peace have not been complex. The largest ethnic group - nearly one-quarter of the US population - turns out to be one of the least visible, a template of assimilation. "I have often thought that the Germans make the best Americans," wrote critic Karl Shapiro, "though they certainly make the worst Germans." German Americans **assimilated** partly because of two world wars with the old country, but also because the Germans who came here - Catholic and Protestants, peasants and city-dwellers - were so diverse. It takes cohesion to stand apart: Germans in American did not have it, and they blended in, leaving only the Katzenjammer Kids behind.

Assimilated take in

English Americans did not have to worry about the melting pot. African Americans, of course, have been in the frying plan or the fire for more than 300 years, while Irish American Catholics, because of their religion and their clannishness, found themselves in a variety of brawls (often with IrishAmerican Protestants). But time has taken down the NO IRISH NEED APPLY signs, and if it doesn't do the same for blacks, it won't be for lack of decades of black and white effort.   racsim?

Will continuing immigration upset the balance? The totals of various Asian groups, though rising rapidly, are still quite small, and it is hard to think of people who seem to be so successful as being difficult to absorb. The real numbers are coming from south of the border. Mexicans are the seventh largest ancestry group, at 11 million, up from 10th place and 7 million in 1980 - a big leap. The census predicts that if today's birthrates hold up (a big if), Hispanics will be nearly a fifth of the US population by 2050. Multiculturalism, now on the doorstep, will have moved in.

But as the census was making this forecast, organizers of a huge private study of Hispanic opinion released some surprising results. The Latino National Political Survey found that the very labels "Hispanic" and "Latino" are rejected by those on whom they are pasted. Americans of Latin American origin think of themselves as urban Americans, Mexican Americans or Puerto Ricans whenever they think in ethnic terms. Mostly they think of joining the American mainstream. Huge majorities of all these groups think residents of the US should learn English, while large majorities - two-thirds or more - think America is admitting too many immigrants. "Hispanics" are going the way of the Germans. By 2050 burritos will be as all-American as Budweiser.

The assimilation of Hispanics is news because two allied groups of political operators are trying to pretend that it isn't happening. Leaders of ethnic communities fear the success of members of their communities because it makes special favors unnecessary and deprives leaders of their status as favor brokers. Meanwhile, liberal believers in the problem-solving omni-competent state mourn any group's graduation from mal-adjustment because it gives them one less thing to do at the office. Both sets of people would protest that they are motivated by idealism and a desire to right wrongs. Always distrust a saint when his charity generates his paychecks.

Talk of mosaics and quilts is both an attempt to describe the way America is headed and an effort to hurry it along. The description is inaccurate, and in a world

200

of un gorgeous mosaics and fraying quilts, the goal is undesirable. The US has had historic success with heavy bursts of immigration, **interspersed** with decades of digestion, but only because people are asked to check their identity at the door. If the mild-mannered Czechs and Slovaks couldn't hold a multiethnic country together, and if the even milder-mannered Canadians are having trouble, we Americans should have second thoughts about becoming a true mosaic. Fortunately we're not one yet, except at the level of boiler plate. Let's hope we never take our speeches seriously

Interspersed
Scattered among other things

MODULE #12

Objectives:

1. Students will be able to read a controversial article and fulfill the requirements of all previous Modules.
2. They will be able to read and write a critique on another student's work, highlighting the strengths of the work and pointing out the weakness or omissions as established in the criteria of all previous Modules.
3. In addition, students will be able to use parallel cases to support their opinions on the controversy.
4. Students will be able to pick out at least three vocabulary words and be able to use them in a sentence.

Assignments:

1. Read "The Myth of Classlessness."
   A. Summarize the article and state the controlling idea and the conflict involved.
   B. Discuss the author's point of view concerning the conflict and describe the component parts of the author's argument.
   C. Give your opinion on the conflict in the article and support your opinion by providing other evidence and parallel cases.
   D. Read a classmate's review of "The Myth of Classlessness" and write a critique pointing out omissions in the analysis or faulty reasoning used by the reviewer.
   E. Flashcard File - 3 words

To him whose elastic and vigorous thought keeps pace with the sun, the day is a perpetual morning.

* Henry David Thoreau

THE MYTH OF CLASSLESSNESS
-Benjamin DeMott

Expatiate
enlarge

This country is in shackles, its thought, character and public policy locked in the distortion and lies. The deceit stands at the root of Federal and state budgetary chaos and corrodes every aspect of national life. It causes the chief executive to **expatiate** on the defense of "our life style" - *our life style* - as though the way of life of the privileged were universal. And that obliviousness is but a minor symptom of a vast, country-wide self-deception.

Icon
symbol

Several hallowed concepts - independence, individualism, choice - are woven into the web of illusion and self-deception. But presiding over the whole is the **icon** of classlessness.

George Bush asserts that class is "for European democracies or something else; it isn't for the United States of America. We are not going to be divided by class." The forces behind this icon of classlessness range from the media to the national experience of public educations.

The myth of classlessness has a history, of course. Caught up in that history, the Framers of the Constitution refused to impose land and property qualifications for Federal office; and 8 out of 10 Americans, in the Depression, claimed to be middle class. In our time, the myth not only lives deep in people's nerves, but exerts an ever more deconstructive influence on public policy.

The myth is in tens of thousands of hours of sitcoms watched by tens of millions, young and old. On "The Cosby Show," black Princeton grads win admission to the law and medical schools of their choice - then chuck it all, preferring to start at the bottom as busboys and waitresses.

Genially
kindly

On "Designing Women," elegant, expensively coifed Southern businesswomen talk for a second or two with striking curtain factory employees and at once become partisans of the strike: "We are all labor!" the ladies cry. In the Harvard alumni magazine, a recent graduate **genially** avers that "we're all working class." And the myth directly affects the distribution of privileges, bounties and hazards in every sector of life.

Every year, a Federal housing donation of close to $40 billion is awarded to millions earning more than $50,000 annually. The donation takes the form of tax

abatements, such as the mortgage interest and property exemptions, and capital gains deferral on housing sales.

Abatements
lessening

The handout to these $50,000-plus neediest comes at a time when the fair market price of rental housing in all 50 states exceeds the means of families in which two wage-earners work full time for the minimum wage, and when New York City alone has 170,000 families on the waiting list for public housing. Only faith that America is a classless society prevents this charity to the properties from being recognized for what it is: an indefensible class rip-off.

And the myth of classlessness figures in corporate decisions that strip the work force of its dignity and skills by killing off one industry after another, from steel to semiconductors. The assumption is that workers aren't shaped by their skills; when quality jobs disappear, workers can just do - and be - something else.

Classlessness functions as the ultimate unspoken excuse for a range of inequities stretching from regressive Social Security taxes to **pauperization** requirements for care of the disable, from Attorney General Dick Thornburgh's rejection of guidelines mandating prison terms for white collar criminals to the denial of proper medical care to heart disease patients lacking private insurance and wholly depending on Medicare

Pauperization
To make poor

The Vietnam "draft," the upper income "bubble," tracking in the public schools, "**vocational**" education - all these episodes of state-administered in justice reflect the influence of the myth of classlessness.

Vocational
Training for
a trade

And always that influence is masked, obscured, down played. Work-related accidents and illnesses kill 70,000 a year - but those people are nearly invisible. "Most occupational risks are blue-collar," says Peter Sandman, director of the Environmental Communication Research Program at Rutgers, "If most risks were professional level, they'd get more (media) coverage."

Gov. James Florio dared to present a fresh, **pertinent** vision of a state prepared to acknowledge the realities of our class system and committed to broadening educational opportunity and narrowing the gulf separating the rich and poor. The protest against his program is strongest in the richest suburbs, but it has significant working class backing. How could it be otherwise, given the huge resources that have been poured into the campaign to persuade us that we're all one, that each has access to all, that serious inequities simply don't exist?

Pertinent
relevant

An immense weight of subsidized opinion has gathered on the side of social untruth, and the means available to those who try to contend against the untruth are fragile. Social wrong is accepted because substantive, as opposed to sitcom, knowledge about class has been habitually suppressed, and the key mode of suppression remains the promotion of the idea of classlessness.

We shall not shake the monster in our midst until we take serious account of the idea of difference - differences between, for one more example, youngsters for whom opportunity means college and youngsters for whom opportunity can only mean the Army. The task is nothing less that that of laying bare the links between the perpetuation of the myth of social sameness and the perpetuation of social wrong. We have all too little time in which to get on with it.

MODULE #13

Objectives:

1. Students will be able to find a controversial article that is local in nature and be able to fulfill all the requirements of the previous modules; local is defined as hometown, county, or state.
2. Students will be able to present orally the issues that are involved in the article and describe the conflict.
3. Students will be able to orally describe all sides of the controversy and to pick one or more of the sides.
4. Students will be able to defend orally their position using any of the techniques found in STEP FIVE, "How to Persuade."
5. Students will be able to pick out at least three vocabulary words and use them in a sentence.
6. Flashcard file - 3 words.

Assignments:

1. Use your library skills
2. Go to the library and find a state or local issue of the newspaper.
   Examples you might want to use:
   > "The controversy over the use of bicycles on the boardwalk in Ocean City." "The Legislature's cutting of the sales tax."

   Sources you might want to use - The Editorial Pages of:
   > Atlantic City Press
   > Mainland Journal
   > Trenton Times

I keep six honest serving men (they taught me all I know). Their names are What, Why and When And How and Where and Who.

* Rudyard Kipling

208

MODULE #14

Objectives:

1. Student will be able to find a controversial issue that is national in nature and be able to fulfill the requirements set in all the previous Modules.
2. Students will be able to present orally the issues that are involved in the article and describe the conflict.
3. Students will be able to describe orally all sides of the controversy and to pick one or more of the sides.
4. Students will be able to defend orally their position using any of the techniques from STEP FIVE, How to Persuade.
5. Students will be able to pick out at least three vocabulary words and use them in a sentence.

Assignments:

1. Use your library skills.
2. Go to the library and find a controversial article that deals with a national issue.
   Examples: Should we have a national health care program?
   Sources you might want to use:
   New York Times
   Newsweek
   US News & World Report
3. Find a second or third article that supports your view of the issue.
4. Write an analysis of each article using the same techniques employed in other modules.

All wish to possess knowledge but few comparatively are willing to pay the price.
* Juvenal

APPENDIX

The Critical Thinker Evaluation Summary Sheet

Assignment   **Points Received**

Module # 1

Module # 2

Module # 3

Module # 4

Module # 5

Module # 6

Module # 7

Module # 8

Module # 9

Module # 10

Module # 11

Module # 12

Module # 13

Module # 14

Bloom's Taxonomy of Educational Objectives
and Verbs for the Objectives

Bloom uses the acronym <u>KCAASE</u> (pronounced case") to identify the key elements in his theory, which describes levels of learning and cognitive activity. KCAASE stands for Knowledge / Comprehension / Application / Analysis/ Synthesis/ Evaluation. The following discussion summarizes this theory.

1. KNOWLEDGE - remembering of previously learned material. The learner knows common terms, specific facts, methods and procedures, basic concepts and principles.

-- defines, describes, identifies, labels, lists, matches, states, selects.

2. COMPREHENSION - ability to grasp the meaning of material. The learner can translate material from one form to another (words to numbers), can explain or summarize, can predict consequences or effects. This level goes beyond remembering and is the lowest level of understanding.

--converts, defends, estimates, explains, gives examples, rewrites –

3. APPLICATION - ability to use learned material in new and concrete situations. The learner demonstrates correct usage of a method of procedure; solves mathematical problems; applies laws and principles to new situations. Learning at this level requires a higher level of understanding than achieved at the comprehension level.

-changes, demonstrates, prepares, solves, uses, operates –

4. ANALYSIS - ability to break down material into its component parts so that its organizational structure may be understood. This may include the identification of the parts, analysis of the relationship of the parts, and the organizational structure of the material.

--breaks down, diagrams, illustrates, subdivides, differentiates

5. SYNTHESIS - ability to put parts together to form a new whole. This may involve the production of a unique plan, a new recipe or menu. This level stresses creative behaviors.

--combines, composes, plans, constructs, writes, devises –

6. EVALUATION - ability to judge the value of material for a given purpose. The judgments of definite criteria. Learning at this level involves elements of all the other levels.

--appraises, criticizes, justifies, compares, contrasts, concludes

A One- Page Condensation of Bloom's Taxonomy of Cognitive Educational Objectives[3]

1.0   Knowledge - <u>Memory</u> objectives calling for the student to <u>recall</u> or recognize Information. Objectives tend to be of one of three types:
1.1 Knowledge of Specifics - specific bits of information
1.2 Knowledge of Ways and Means of Dealing with Specifics – organizing
1.3 1.3 Knowledge of Universals and Abstractions - theories and generalizations

2.0   Comprehension — <u>Understanding</u> objectives which go beyond remembering to being able to perform certain operations with a communication beyond recalling or reproducing it. There are three categories.
2.1 Translation - Objectives calling for the student to change information into a different symbolic form of language, i.e, rephrase.
2.2 Interpretation - Objectives in which the student is required not only to rephrase, but to explain or give the meaning of the communication,
2.3 Extrapolation - Objectives requiring a student to make certain predictions or draw certain implications that go beyond given data.

3.0   Application - <u>Transfer</u> objectives calling for a student to apply what he knows, Le. solve a life like problem that requires the identification of the issue and the selection and use of appropriate generalizations and skills.

4.0   Analysis - Objectives in which a student takes a whole and breaks it down into its parts. There are three classifications:
4.1 Analysis of elements
4.2 Analysis of relationships
4.3 Analysis of organizational principles

5.0   Synthesis - <u>Creativity</u> objectives calling for the student to create a new whole out of the parts that are available.
Or
Solve a problem that calls for original, creative thinking. Three kinds:
5.1 Production of a unique communication - communicating to others
5.2 Production of a plan or proposed set of operations.
5.3 Derivation of a set of abstract relations - formulating hypotheses or propositions.

6.0   Evaluation - Judging objectives calling for the student to make a quantitative or qualitative judgment according to criteria previously learned. Judgments are of two types:
6.1 Judgments in terms of internal evidence - logical accuracy, internal consistency, etc.
6.2 Judgments in terms of external criteria - evaluation of internal data to outside influences and selected criteria.

---

[3] Adapted from Benjamin S. Bloom. et. al. <u>Taxonomy of Educational Objectives. Handbook I Cognitive Domain.</u> New York: David McKay Co., 1956.